Rules of the Game

Lessons from the Field
of Community Change

ABOUT THE AUTHOR

Mark S. Homan has been a full-time faculty member in the Social Services Department of Pima Community College since 1978; he has been the chairman of the department for the past several years. In addition to his duties at Pima, Mark has served as an adjunct faculty member in the Department of Sociology and Social Work at Northern Arizona University and in the Graduate School of Social Work at Arizona State University. He received his M.S.W. from Arizona State University in 1975 and is a certified independent social worker in the state of Arizona.

A strong advocate of community empowerment, Mark continues to use his very active involvement in the community to contribute to its improvement and to enhance his own learning. For 25 years he has worked with diverse populations in urban, rural, and reservation communities on a broad range of issues, including neighborhood stabilization and empowerment, hunger, reproductive rights, children with special health needs, family planning, capital punishment, public schools and community development, political campaign organizing, foster care, and adoption. In addition to his roles as organizer, lobbyist, consultant, and teacher, Mark has developed and directed several human services programs. He has also been a founding member of many community organizations and agencies and has served on numerous community boards and councils.

Mark is the author of *Promoting Community Change: Making It Happen in the Real World,* Second Edition, a textbook that has been used in colleges and universities throughout the country as well as by public and private groups. He has conducted many workshops and delivered numerous presentations dealing with various aspects of community building and community power. He is frequently asked by public and private organizations to assist them in increasing their effectiveness.

Mark serves on the editorial board of the journal *Human Service Education.* He is the recipient of the President's Award from the National Organization for Human Service Education,

At this stage in his career Mark has finally come to recognize that he will not be playing shortstop for the San Francisco Giants.

Rules of the Game

Lessons from the Field
of Community Change

Mark S. Homan

Brooks/Cole Publishing Company

 An International Thomson Publishing Company

Pacific Grove • Albany • Belmont • Bonn • Boston • Cincinnati • Detroit • Johannesburg • London
Madrid • Melbourne • Mexico City • New York • Paris • Singapore • Tokyo • Toronto • Washington

Acquisitions Editor: *Lisa I. Gebo*
Marketing Team: *Steve Catalano,*
    Jean Thompson, Aaron Eden
Editorial Assistant: *Susan Wilson*
Production Editor: *Nancy L. Shammas*
Production Service: *Anne Draus,*
    Scratchgravel Publishing Services
Permissions Editor: *May Clark*

Manuscript Editor: *Kay Mikel*
Cover Photo: *Ian Christie/The Stock Market*
Cover Design: *F. tani Hasegawa*
Typesetting: *Scratchgravel Publishing*
    Services
Printing and Binding: *Webcom*

For more information, contact:

BROOKS/COLE PUBLISHING COMPANY
511 Forest Lodge Road
Pacific Grove, CA 93950
USA

International Thomson Publishing Europe
Berkshire House 168-173
High Holborn
London WC1V 7AA
England

Thomas Nelson Australia
102 Dodds Street
South Melbourne, 3205
Victoria, Australia

Nelson Canada
1120 Birchmount Road
Scarborough, Ontario
Canada M1K 5G4

International Thomson Editores
Seneca 53
Col. Polanco
115060 México, D. F., México

International Thomson Publishing GmbH
Königswinterer Strasse 418
53227 Bonn
Germany

International Thomson Publishing Asia
60 Albert Street
#15-01 Albert Complex
Singapore 189969

International Thomson Publishing Japan
Hirakawacho Kyowa Building, 3F
2-2-1 Hirakawacho
Chiyoda-ku, Tokyo 102
Japan

Printed in Canada

10 9 8 7 6 5 4 3 2 1

Library of Congress Cataloging-in-Publication Data

Homan, Mark S., [date]–
    Rules of the game : lessons from the field of community change /
Mark S. Homan.
        p. cm.
    Includes bibliographic references (p.   ).
    ISBN 0-534-35871-3 (alk. paper)
    1. Community leadership.   2. Community development.   3. Community
organization.   I. Title.
HN49.C6H645   1998
307.1'4—dc21   98-7950
                                                                          CIP

To those special parents of children with special strengths,
whose love, dignity, and commitment
have taught me so much.

And to the residents of Rincon Heights,
who together stood taller
than the giant they faced.

Contents

Preface

This book is written for people who have decided that "the way things are" just isn't good enough. These people no longer want to put up with things that need to be changed. When you make a commitment to make a difference, you want your actions to produce the results you intend. You want to have some idea of what you need to do to make things work out. *Rules of the Game* was written for you.

To some extent the field of community change is like a game. You have players. You have goals. You have motivation. You even can have some fun. The game is less frustrating and easier to play if you understand the rules. The first rule is: *There are no rules.* There is no magic formula, no prescription for success, no cookbook to follow. Whatever change you are cooking up will look different from all the others.

That's a great start, isn't it? If there are no rules, then what is in this book? Some pretty good direction. Most of these principles apply most of the time. However, the combination you need and how you emphasize these principles will vary from change effort to change effort. What you need to do will be shaped by the demands of your experience and the resources you have at your disposal. These principles will help you pay attention to the things you need to do, and they will guide you as you do them.

The Rules of the Game are based on reflections of my own experience covering more than 20 years of work with diverse groups to produce change in a variety of circumstances. These have included urban neighborhood organizing, legislative action, rural community development, community action around issues such as hunger, and the establishment of social services programs, to name a few. Whenever I am working to promote change, I take some time to try to figure out what is or is not working and why. These rules and the Essential Eight steps for building an organization were born of such figuring. They were created during a time of action, then reconsidered and honed for future use. Those that survived the test were added to this list.

So, what you will be reading did not come about because I sat down to write a book. These are not after-the-fact ideas. The Rules of the Game were jotted down at the moment of awareness, during the action. The book came about because these tips, originally written as reminders to me, were collected over time. They are a direct result of some activity that produced an insight into the process of change.

I use these rules all the time. I wish I had known them when I was first getting started. I know I need to clearly observe them in my work today. From time to time, when I seem to be stuck, I take them out of my back pocket to see which I am taking for granted and which I need to pay more attention to. I add to them still, and I continue to refine them just a bit. So, although these principles may be particularly useful for those of you who are fairly new to this endeavor, they should serve as important reminders for those of you with more experience as well.

While writing this book, I kept in mind the faces of the people with whom I have worked, people who were intending to make things better for themselves and for others in their communities. In most cases they were not sure of themselves when they started out, and they didn't have much power. As I set about explaining each rule or step in building an organization, I found myself looking into Becky's face or Marvin's or maybe Amy's, trying to see if what I was writing would have made sense to them when they first started. Would these rules make sense to them now that they have learned and taught others? I think the answer is yes. These rules are for the people who will use them.

The principles and tips described here may provide some new discoveries or serve as important reminders for experienced, full-time activists, but they are particularly offered to those who do not have years of experience working toward changes in their communities. College students, having considered abstract notions in the classroom regarding communities and community change, can now bring those ideas to life in meaningful practice. Neighborhood leaders can bring residents together to strengthen bonds and improve conditions for individuals and families. Workers in social service agencies and schools can create more powerful responses to change harmful conditions rather than learning to accept them. Leaders of faith communities can energize their congregations to confront social injustice. Health care workers can help to build vital communities that provide for the health of their members.

The rules are written to you as a change agent. You may not be the single most visible leader in an organization, but you are actively involved in figuring out the direction of some aspect of the effort and in contributing to the work that needs to be done.

Many, many of the partners with whom I have worked ended up playing significant roles in a change effort, although in a few cases that was not their original intent. Those of you who do not currently play a leading role will find these ideas useful as you become more assertively involved. Many of these principles can assist you even when your sphere of responsibility in a change episode is fairly small. The notions that don't immediately apply to you will give you some guidance as you grow into greater leadership responsibilities. Those of you who now perform a major leadership function will routinely practice these concepts as you use your position to strengthen the organization and move closer to your goals.

I will speak directly to you, the reader, throughout these pages. I want you to put yourself into the change agent's role. Think about what you might do when working with others to promote change. You cannot help if you stand outside the action observing what other people might have done or might be doing. This book is full of guidelines for action.

I want to make one extremely important clarification regarding the word *you*, a word found on every page of this book. When I refer to "you" or "your goals" or "your organization," I am speaking both to you and to the people working with you. I do not intend to imply that your are a single individual acting alone, or that you are a leader with a bunch of obedient followers. You don't own the organization, but you have a stake in it, along with others. So, when I refer to "you," I am referring to you working with others or the collective "you" of your organization.

Part I consists of two chapters. Chapter 1 describes the guiding principles that successful change agents draw on to direct their work. The more conscious you are of these basic concepts, the more you will be able to make sense out of what is going on. Then you will be better equipped to recognize potential opportunities and challenges as you determine avenues for effective action. The specific steps involved in promoting community change are described in Chapter 2, "The Essential Eight." Here you will be introduced to the sequence of activities you need to undertake to promote change. You will also learn about concepts that are at work in each phase in the process. Key questions must be asked at each step along the way, and your answers will provide direction for completing that step and guiding you to the next one.

The Rules of the Game themselves constitute Part II of the book. Each rule highlights a specific insight on some particular aspect of the change process. The rules in Chapter 3 illustrate some basic things to know about this business of change. Chapter 4 helps you take a look at yourself as a change agent and better understand the things you can do to be effective, or the things you may do that get in your own way. Chapter 5 provides a keener understanding of ways to strengthen the approaches you take when trying to produce change. The final set of rules, those contained in Chapter 6, considers things you should know about the people involved in a change effort.

Part III sets forth the "Thirteen Commandments of Community Change." These commandments encompass fundamental precepts of community change. They serve as final reminders of the things you need to know and do as an agent of change.

The rules and other principles described in this book recognize that most of the work of groups seeking change is done by people who are volunteering to do it. Many of these people are not yet convinced that they can make a meaningful contribution to the effort. Often they are not even convinced that their effort will succeed in changing anything. I have written *Rules of the Game* because what we do as change agents matters. We bring about a little more dignity and a little more comfort, and we all benefit. Congratulations and thank you.

Acknowledgments

I have gained from the wisdom and guidance of the many people with whom I have worked over the years. Although it is impossible to include here all who have taught and encouraged me, I do want to particularly thank two. I especially appreciate Lee Hunter, manager of the Arizona Department of Health Services Community Development Initiative, whose questions have helped me learn and whose deep sense of purpose has challenged me. The thoughtful critique and insights of Ann Nichols of Arizona State University have guided me to a stronger understanding of the principles of change and the meaning of integrity.

I also want to thank those who reviewed drafts of what would become this book. Their thoughtful comments helped me to rethink or rephrase critical points. They are: Becky Hamblin, Alliance for Children and Families of Southern Apache County; Ann W. Nichols, Arizona State University; Dennis Poole, University of Central Florida; and Patrick Romine, University of Phoenix.

Ultimately it has been those citizens who have believed in the possibility of a finer future and their responsibility in shaping it who have helped put these ideas to the test and refine them through action.

I have received important assistance and support from many at Pima Community College, especially Richard Fridena, Alvin Lewis, Tommie

Miller, Luba Chliwniak, Rosaisela Valenzuela, Diana Montano, Beth Doyle, Sheila Hughes, Mike Curry, and Jo Namsick.

Once again the members of the Brooks/Cole team have shown their multiple talents in helping me bring this project to a better conclusion. I have benefited greatly from the professionalism and support of Lisa Gebo, Nancy Shammas, and Susan Wilson. Anne Draus of Scratchgravel Publishing Services has lent her expertise in keeping the project on track. Kay Mikel, who with her sharp pencil has reined in my recalcitrant prose, deserves special thanks.

My family has provided me so much throughout this project—and many others. Your patience, humor, and love sustain me and keep me well rooted.

Mark S. Homan

Rules of the Game

**Lessons from the Field
of Community Change**

PART I

Getting Started

CHAPTER 1

Guiding Principles for Change Agents

Community change comes in all sizes, and all of it matters. You matter. The people who toil with you in your work community matter. The people who live in your neighborhood matter. The people who go to school with your children or who take classes with you or who are sick and hungry and invisible matter. You all matter.

Your decision to work for change recognizes this truth. Your decision to work effectively honors it. So, you will ask questions of yourself and of others who might have something to offer. You will observe and reflect. You will learn about the specific situation you are trying to improve, and you will learn as much as you can about the business of promoting change.

I have found certain guiding principles useful in directing the work of community change. These concepts form the foundation for the Essential Eight, the Rules of the Game, and even the Thirteen Commandments. Change efforts that are strongly rooted in an understanding of these principles will have a good chance to grow.

Community change includes any purposeful effort to improve a condition that exists in a community. These conditions can be very local, such as changing one set of practices in one particular school, or they can be more far reaching, such as developing community resources to reduce crime.

Your actions as an agent of change will affect people immediately within your reach and many others whom you may never know at all. Your decisions will alter the way the community functions, moving it toward a greater degree of health for the benefit of all its members. Even if the changes you pursue seem minor, this is a very noble thing to do.

Healthy communities tend to produce healthy people, and distressed and depressed communities tend to produce distressed and depressed people. People necessarily must make adaptations to survive within the environment in which they live. A constellation of forces are present in any community. Some of these forces may be harmful, but a number of them can be beneficial. These forces can include physical elements, such as pure water, or less visible influences, such as racism. Members of the community feel the effects of these forces, sometimes directly, sometimes only slightly. Communities deteriorate when their members must continually contend ineffectively with an overwhelming set of harmful forces, and each person is diminished. Communities are invigorated when their members benefit from shared access to healthy forces, and each person becomes stronger.

Healthy communities are inclusive communities.   Healthy communities recognize that each of their members has value and has interests. Inclusive communities challenge themselves to discover and make use of that value and to meet legitimate interests. They don't give up easily, and they don't capitulate to the politics of exclusion when relationships among members become difficult.

Engaged communities are healthy communities.   Communities in which members are actively engaged with one another and with what might be called community life create a series of interlocking relationships with one another and with the whole. These overlapping networks of relationships become a particular resource, a source of wealth to the community, that provides members with various sources of support. When maintenance of relationships is valued and isolation is uncommon, community members are much less likely to exploit or to be exploited. Engaged communities have higher levels of trust and provide their participants with numerous opportunities for collaboration, with the consequent recognition and development of individual and community resources. Participants in such communities act to preserve and enhance community identity and strengthen the way the community functions.

Each community has assets that need to be recognized, developed, and used.
Few communities have everything they need to accomplish their goals, but many of them have much of what they need—and all have enough to get started. Too often, communities and the change agents working in them focus on what they *do not* have rather than on what they *do* have. Although stoking the irritation of unmet need can be a good way to stir the desire for action, it doesn't do much to promote progress. To the desire for action must be added the means for taking action. The means are found in the community's assets. These are what you build on.

Your use of a skill, like speaking a different language or playing a musical instrument, strengthens it. In a similar way, the more you practice using a community's resources, the more fully developed these resources will become. Communities that mobilize their own assets come to see themselves as more capable. They begin to recognize more and more of their assets as well.

Communities of any size operate as a system, which is made up of smaller systems and is itself part of a larger system.   You might think of a community system as an organism that must continually act to maintain a healthy condition. Systems tend to have a number of characteristics.

First, a system needs input, which the system uses to sustain its life, and which it converts into some sort of product or waste. For example, you yourself are a system. One of your sources of input is food, which your body uses to nourish itself, converting some of that food into energy so that you can go about your productive daily tasks, which may include getting more food.

Second, each system must relate effectively to its environment. A system must get from the environment what it needs and give back to the environment to help that host environment to function.

Third, a system must achieve some sort of balance so that it can effectively take care of routine demands. A system that is unstable or out of balance will act erratically, paying much more attention to some things while ignoring others.

Finally, any system is comprised of an interrelationship of smaller systems, or component parts, and each system itself is a component part of an even larger system. This means that what happens in one part of the system to some extent affects the entire system, much like you hitting your thumb with a hammer affects much more than just your thumb. It will probably affect your entire hand, your heart rate, and the way your stomach feels, not to mention your general outlook on life at that moment. The system must take care of its component parts to remain healthy. Further, what happens outside of the system, in the larger environment, can affect the health of the system.

By looking at a community as a system you can begin to recognize its component parts (each one itself a system) and how it takes care of them. You can begin to better understand how the community relates to the larger environment. You can see that it needs to bring in money, or information, or other forms of input to keep it operating in a healthy way. It needs to use those forms of input to properly take care of itself and become productive. You can also start to understand that one small part of the system can get the system's attention and cause it to respond.

In short, you can get a better grasp on the situation to determine ways that the community can strengthen or weaken itself. This understanding provides you with some avenues for action.

Generation of and use of power sufficient for the issue at hand are essential for producing change. Essentially, power is energy that is put to use. In the field of community change, it is energy put to use to get people to respond so that the effect of their response leads to a change in the way things are. That is, people begin to feel, to think, and ultimately to act in new or different ways. They respond by passing new laws, by changing business practices, or perhaps by working in collaborative ways. The whole point of community change is to change what people do, how they do it, and the structures that influence these things. The use of power makes that happen.

Power comes from many different sources. It can be in the form of information or votes or voices. It can be physical strength or money. Even the willingness to comply is a form of power. Any resource, including an action, that is needed in a given circumstance provides a source of power, whereas a resource that is not needed provides little, if any, power. If you are stranded in the middle of the desert, whose resource do you most need at that time, your friend with the canteen full of water or your friend with the twenty dollar bill?

A change agent needs to be mindful of the many, many sources of power at her or his disposal. Enough of this power must be brought together and then focused at the right point to produce the response that is needed. The bigger the issue, the more power you will need. Breaking the issue down into smaller parts will help you focus the power you have. In all cases the extent of your power must be greater than the size of the issue or the part of the issue you are working on. And in all cases, you must actually use your power for it to do any good.

Selection of a particular strategic approach should be made intentionally. Your choice of strategy reflects your decision on how your power can best be used. Strategies that are the results of conscious choices to meet the demands of the situation are much more likely to succeed than those that are products of reaction. Your choice of which strategy to pursue involves understanding the nature of the issue, the nature of the opposition, the nature of your support, and your ability to acquire additional resources.

Everything depends on people taking action and people responding to that action. By taking action, and only by taking action, you set things in motion and begin to assert some direction over the course of events.

These actions create imbalance, some new set of forces to which the system must respond to establish a new sense of equilibrium. It is through action that the issue is brought to the attention of key actors in the community, and it is through action that additional supporters are attracted and emboldened. Only when people begin acting and responding does change begin to take place.

Significant empowerment occurs within the context of community, not apart from it. Connecting people to one another and to the issue is a critical component of power building. You will work in partnership with other people, sometimes in a leadership role, sometimes not. Although you may initiate change, acting alone you will accomplish little. The notion that one person creates change is naive and arrogant. An individual complains, keeping his or her discomforts in some way separate from the concerns of others. A change agent mobilizes the concerns and contributions of a sufficient number of others to establish new, healthier patterns of community life. Together all of you participate in making change happen.

People become truly more powerful by being in relationships with others who have a common identity and a common purpose. This type of power is much more substantial and much more sustainable than individual power. An individual can learn skills for acting personally more powerfully, but that power is often limited to immediate transactions or narrowly defined circumstances. Personal power is amplified and supported through participation in a community where that same person becomes linked to the many sources of power that exist there. The mere fact of being accepted and included in a larger whole is empowering. Beyond that, when people act with others in concert and on purpose, each individual's power is increased.

Maintaining interest, involvement, and productive relationships among participants requires ongoing attention. Interest, involvement, and productive relationships cannot be taken for granted, for each is always in a process of growth or decline. As a change agent, these matters become part of your routine orientation. Get into the habit of looking at everything through the lens of strengthening participant interest, involvement, and relationships. You cannot attend to these matters just when you have the time. And you will soon realize that you cannot avoid these matters, because every activity of the change effort affects them one way or the other.

The work of the change effort is held together and intensified by an ever-growing sense of investment from a growing number of people. Paying purposeful attention to this is a main part of the change agent's job.

A clear, compelling issue is necessary to ignite interest and provide a focus.
Without a specific issue for people to rally around, a change effort can
very easily lose a sense of direction—precisely because, without a clear
issue, the direction is not very clear. The issue unifies the energy and the
identity of the group. It helps participants stay on track.

A good issue touches people in a way that provokes an emotional response. A good issue also provides a way to perceive and define a situation in a way that suggests clarity of purpose and clarity of action.

***Effective change agents recognize that cultural differences exist and affirm
those differences.***   People from distinct cultural groups have different
perspectives, experiences, expectations, knowledge, and other qualities
or attributes. These differences can become a source of conflict, separa-
tion, and debilitation if they are unheeded or disregarded. They can become a source of harmony, richness, and strength when they are recognized and valued. A change agent with an appreciation of cultural
diversity can communicate more effectively, make more relevant decisions, and capitalize more fully on a broader range of insights and
talents.

A number of different cultural groups help shape our views and our
behaviors. Many groups have strong rituals, standards, customs, and
specialized knowledge. In addition to ethnicity, cultural groups also include professional, activity, or geographic communities. Attachments to
our various cultural identities differ, and the attachments that members
of a particular culture feel differ as well. In many cases culture provides
identity, a sense of belonging and nurturance, which can support community life.

Organizations go through understandable stages of development.   You know
that the organization of a change effort doesn't burst forth suddenly into
full flower, yet hidden in some corner of your eagerness and enthusiasm
is a feeling that it should. As a change agent, you may have to rein in
some impatience and handle some degree of frustration as well. Your organization is likely to go through a series of stages.

In the *introduction* stage you and others recognize a need for action,
become acquainted with the issues and with each other, and decide to
act. In the next stage, *initial action,* you begin gathering information, increasing the number of supporters, and generally performing a number
of tasks required to complete a particular action. Next comes the *emergence of leadership and structure stage,* as the group learns who it can rely
on or as particular members begin to assert themselves. As the group

recognizes that it needs to gain a clearer focus and act more efficiently, some routine ways for handling predictable tasks and making decisions are developed. This is frequently followed by a *letdown, loss of members, and floundering stage,* as the initial energy gives way to more tedious tasks; mistakes (of others) are more readily noted and less readily tolerated, and risks, including risks of failure, heighten insecurity. Any lack of clarity or mutuality of goals becomes more evident at this stage, and it is not uncommon for members to begin bickering. This stage, like all the others, is normal, but if members, especially leaders, don't recognize that fact, the organization may not progress past this stage. In the next stage, *recommitment, new tasks, and new members,* the group makes adjustments and leadership asserts itself to provide direction, confidence, and motivation. Renewed dedication brings new participants. This is generally followed by a period of *sustained action* as the group continues its work and makes and notices progress. More structure emerges at this stage, and the group is willing to take on more challenges. Finally, the group moves toward *continued growth, decline, or termination.* Growth often occurs by repeating the previous phases in a more efficient manner than the first time. Decline generally results when new challenges or new resources are not developed. Termination of the effort follows from successful completion of a specific project or from unsuccessful efforts (often inattention) to reverse a decline.

Any organization will typically go through these stages. While your group is in one dominant stage, it is likely to be engaged concurrently in several stages as it moves through one and prepares for another. If you can recognize the signs that your group is dealing with normal developmental challenges, you can help to keep yourselves from getting stuck.

Change requires new movement in a new direction.   Going from the known to the unknown, rejecting accommodation, courting rejection, and taking a chance on a better tomorrow are often not particularly comfortable. Learning the moves to a very different dance when there are few, if any, around to teach you, can be a little intimidating for some. Most of us learned to dance by first stumbling around a bit. Most experienced change agents did too. We paid attention to the direction we were supposed to be moving, and now things seem much more natural.

Change involves risk taking. Some of these risks are imagined, but some are very real. All change agents experience some degree of trepidation. All change agents also feel some degree of doubt throughout the life of the change effort. When you feel these things, recognize them as normal.

The attraction of the unknown can be at once exciting and unnerving. For those who more easily accept the challenge to promote change, it may be difficult to be patient with those for whom uncertainty is a greater foe. Change agents need to recognize that some question of confidence is always at hand when trying to produce change. So an effective change agent will cultivate trust and self-reliance, along with a taste for adventure. Helping a group of people move into the unknown is one of the change agent's biggest tests.

The change agent receives ultimate direction from the community.   First, I want to make an extremely important clarification; one that those of you with experience well understand that I need to make. When I refer to "you" or "your goals" or "your organization," I am speaking of both you and the people working with you. I do not intend to imply that you are a single individual acting alone, nor that you are a leader with just a bunch of obedient followers. You don't own the organization, but you have a stake in it—so do many others. So when I refer to "you," I am referring to you working with others or the collective "you" of your organization.

As a result, you are working with a community rather than having a community working with you. The change agent must listen to the community as well as offer direction. It is the community who must act, not just the change agent, and the final decisions will always reside with the community. After all, whose change is it anyway?

A good change agent is in many ways a good teacher.   Ultimately, all good teachers are students who can learn from their partners in learning and from the world around them. You (and I) will never really know it all. This is at once a frustrating and an exciting proposition. You will need to reflect on your actions and your intended actions. Out of this will come your own creativity and discovery. Out of this will come your increased skill and confidence. Out of this will come your own Rules of the Game.

You will find little esoteric mystery here. Much of the success of community change can be traced to common sense recognized, remembered, and acted upon. As you read, I hope you will recognize these dominant, recurring themes, which find expression in numerous aspects of any effort to promote change. Some of the principles described in the following pages are self-evident. However, experienced change agents know that they are not applied consistently enough in practice. They may be what we understand. They must become what we do.

CHAPTER 2

The Essential Eight: An Outline for Community Change

The various Rules of the Game are like snapshots you take to remember the action. They are not the action itself but important parts frozen in mid-moment to enable you to look more closely at what is occurring there. You can ponder over these snapshots to appreciate more fully the events taking place. Yet to understand the game, you need to have a sense of its flow, how one set of actions leads to another, sometimes in clear sequence, sometimes in apparent simultaneity. The story evolves in motion.

Promoting Purposeful Change

In this section you can begin to see how the pieces fit into place. You will learn how to move from discomfort to progress. Although the steps identified here describe a process for beginning a change effort, these are also the very same basic procedures used to sustain it.

The real world is not always as orderly as the world you imagine when you determine the direction of your action. It certainly does not present itself in as convenient and predictable a way as I will describe here. Yet the real world does offer some room for maneuvering and some time to progress from one thing to the next. This is an important understanding. Some events may seem to move you ahead a few spaces, and others may keep you stuck. However, this is not a reason to abandon your efforts to haphazard chance. You have some influence on the nature and the course of events that affect you, and you can increase your influence by acting in a purposeful way. So do the best you can, understanding that the world may not know of the orderly and rational progression of activities you have prepared for it.

Intended results are produced by actions that are sufficiently purposeful and powerful. This implies both design and ability. Without both of these, outcomes are either random or insufficient. That is, if you do not have a sense of what you want to achieve nor how to achieve it, any positive consequences are more or less accidental. Also, if you do not have the power, the necessary resources to act on your intentions, you may achieve only a portion of what you had planned. The process described in the following pages recognizes the necessity for purposeful, powerful action.

Before we begin, a couple of basic notions about working for change are helpful to consider. *When you are working for change, everything you do is geared to getting some response from some identified person or set of persons*. Purposeful change occurs when your actions introduce something different into the immediate environment—something that changes that environment and causes others to respond to these new conditions by behaving differently. As someone who intends to promote change, you do this on purpose. Stripped down to its essentials, planned change means that people are acting differently because you (and other members of your community) want them to. Always remember this simple point: You do what you do to get people to do what you want them to do.

I realize that upon first reading, this statement may sound harsh, even manipulative. When you think about it though, when is this not true when working for change? When do you not want your actions to produce a response? Your intention is to stop people from doing something, such as despoiling the environment or exploiting the poor. Or your intention is to start people doing something, such as including those who have been excluded or offering protection to those who are at risk or building a new bridge. Your intent is that your actions will lead to people doing things differently. Whether or not this is manipulative is left up to your view of people, your motives, and the actions you decide to take. But keep this clearly in mind: You are always looking to produce a response.

This raises some very fundamental questions. Who are these people? What response do you want from them? What actions are you able to take that can provoke this response? When do you need to take these actions? What will you do after you do or do not get your intended response? Your work for change is shaped in large part by your answers to these questions.

A design begins to take form when you consider the goals you have in mind and the responses from people that are necessary for the members of your community to achieve that goal. For your group to be effective, it will need to be able to develop and direct resources in a very concentrated way. *Change occurs when you are able to focus your power at critical times on critical people in a critical way.*

Accumulating resources is fundamental in expanding your options for action and promoting your ability to move effectively into actions you have decided to take. Resources provide a base of power. These resources could be numbers of people and their talents and connections, information, media attention, or anything else that can produce a needed response. When you prepare to act, you must ask yourself two questions: *What do we have that we can use to influence the people we need to influence?* and *How can we get more of what we need?*

Having assets is one thing. Using them effectively is another. This speaks to organization. *An effective change effort is sustained by an effective organization.* Whether the change you seek is small or far reaching, you will need to develop some sort of organization. Any group of people that works together to accomplish a goal can be seen as an organization. Though some of these organizations exist in only the most rudimentary way, each has some degree of leadership, confidence, enthusiasm, skill building, and management of tasks, along with other essentials depending on the nature and complexity of the challenges faced. The actions the organization takes should allow it to continue to increase its strengths and use them in an efficient, productive way.

As a change agent, you consciously act to produce three results: (1) to make headway toward your goal, (2) to help accumulate resources that you will be able to put to use, and (3) to increase the ability of your organization to function effectively.

One final set of questions must be asked to ensure that your efforts remain clear and meaningful: What are these actions intended to produce? How do these results move us toward our goal? How do these actions provide us with more resources? How does this action develop our organization? And one final check: Is everything we are doing related to the outcomes we want to produce?

The Essential Eight

The process of change revolves around the *Essential Eight*—eight elements for moving from inaction to accomplishment. These elements may be seen as a progression of steps that the change agent takes, moving from one phase of the change effort into the next. As the Rules of the Game presented later might suggest, obviously there is much more to this business of promoting change than what can be captured by the Essential

Eight. However, all that additional information is by and large either an elaboration of these elements or further directions on their application.

You can best understand the Essential Eight as a primer or an outline for action. Once you master these elements, you will have a very good handle on the core activities required for you to be a successful change agent.

One: Decide to Act with Purpose

This is a critical first step. It moves you past irritation, past hoping, past worrying, past complaining, past all those forms of wanting somebody else to make things better for you. The more clear your decision, the more ready you will be to take on the responsibility for effective action. In addition, you will be less resistant to doing the work you know needs doing. You will not do the minimum, and you will not drive yourself silly in a bluster of random actions trying to accomplish everything at once.

The decision to act cannot be purely rational but must rise out of a flame of some desire. Everything is based on this decision. Pushing through the barriers that give comfort to inaction is one of the most difficult and noble things you can do.

You must make this decision more than once. You will face a number of barriers after you have begun your work. If you pay diligent attention to the Essential Eight, the re-decision for purposeful action will be more easily made. It is worth repeating—everything is based on this decision.

Key Questions for Deciding to Act with Purpose
- Are you deciding to make a difference, or are you just going along with someone else's decision?
- Do you anticipate some unexpected setbacks?
- Do you know you need to build the interest and commitment of other people and that you will need to make room for their contributions, including their leadership?
- Do you anticipate that you will be able to recognize progress, even when the going is slow?
- Are you willing to take some satisfaction from the good things that happen, including your decision to act in the first place?
- Are you willing to learn what you need to know?

Two: Understand and Clarify the Issue

What do you know about this condition you want to change? Have you found a specific issue to focus on? What do you know about this issue? A halfhearted investment in having a firm grasp of the issue will limit you. You will be halted by your ignorance and your inability to articulate your concerns. You will be caught off guard or you will be unsure of yourself. The opposite is also true. Having a solid handle on the matter will give you confidence and strength. You will be able to counter ignorance and deception. You will be able to educate and spark interest.

Almost every step in the change process requires some degree of homework, some commitment to finding out more. This is certainly true when it comes to the very matter that has provoked you to act. The questions in this and the following sections require more than some reflection. They require you to do some digging and analyzing, followed by more digging and more analyzing. Again, as with every other step, the quality of what you produce will increase dramatically when you work with other people. Your collective discoveries and conversations about your discoveries will help you to shape what is compelling for people to know about the issue and how they can come to know it.

Key Questions for Understanding and Clarifying the Issue
- What is the source of discomfort about this issue? (Remember, "discomfort" can include something exciting that people want to create or do. The tension existing between the current condition and that new exciting one is a kind of discomfort.)
- What is the nature and extent of discomfort?
- What is it that you want to be different?
- What basic assumptions about decency or fairness or some other widely held values does this involve?

These questions will help you look at the effect or implications of this condition or issue:

- What are the legal implications, especially related to the denial of rights?
- What are the financial consequences, especially what scarcities, losses, or added expenses may result?
- What are the effects on society, the community, or a particular group?
- What impact does this condition have for individual people?

Consider some alternative approaches to the current management of the issue.

- How has this matter been handled elsewhere?
- What solutions or better responses can be developed?
- What does "better" look like?

Never let these questions be far from your consideration.

*   Do you know what you are talking about?
*   What are the consequences of your answer?

You will never know everything about the issue, although you do need to know a sufficient amount to have confidence when you are doing your work. You will continue to learn more about the issue throughout the life of the change effort as new action yields new information and insight. Again, this is true for every element in the process. You will learn more about every phase by acting on it.

You will be aided in your pursuit of information and your ability to rally people by identifying a clear, identifiable issue. This could be some particular point or aspect about the condition that you would like to change. The earlier you are in the change process, the more immediate and specific this issue should be. For example, if you are dealing with traffic in a neighborhood, you might focus on a specific issue such as speed or a specific action such as putting a stop sign on a dangerous corner. If you are working on conditions in the schools for children with special health care needs, you might focus on the way Individual Educational Plans are developed and reviewed or the availability of a classroom aide.

With an increased command of the issue you will be able to articulate it compellingly. You will be able to strike something that your audience of potential supporters cares about—children, money, security, forfeiture of their rights, or some other concern. You will feel secure in your point of view and be willing to assert it.

Replay these beginning and ending questions: What do you know about this issue? What else do you need to know?

Three: Know the Actors in the Play

Remember that this whole notion of community change is fundamentally about people and what they feel, think, and do. It is people who provide opposition as well as support. What you intend to do will touch a number of people other than yourself. The greater the change you seek, the more people who will be affected. Who are these people, and what role do you see them playing in the drama you want to help produce?

It is from this field that you will draw the people you most assuredly need to help secure the change. This is also where you will find people who are willing to change their minds, those who refuse to do so, and those who just can't seem to make up their minds. The reasons for people's responses to the invitation you offer are rooted in their perspective on the scene. These perspectives are directed by their perception of their interests. By giving some clear thought to the people and the interests involved in the situation you intend to change, you are better able to gauge what people are likely or unlikely to do. This is an imperfect process because some people have interests that apparently conflict. Even that can be a valuable discovery; that tension may provide some opportunity for flexibility. Your awareness of the sort of responses you can predict or encourage will be invaluable in determining your strategies and tactics.

Although it is appropriate to consider classes of people, such as faculty or parents or the people living in the Sunset Terrace apartment building, individual people with individual names merit your attention as well.

The next series of questions will help you determine whom you need to take into account. You will notice that many of the questions relate to each other and that there is some degree of overlap. It is helpful to get into the practice of seeing the same situation from a number of different angles.

Key Questions for Knowing the Actors in the Play
- Whom does this issue touch most directly?
- Whom does it touch indirectly?
- Who feels the problem?
- Who benefits from the problem?
- Whose behavior needs to change?
    Among those who don't feel the problem?
    Among those who feel the problem?
- Who makes decisions on matters affecting this issue? What contacts do you have with any of these people?
- Who maintains the problem?
    Those who officially support it through some formal authority (for example, through maintenance of harmful policies)?
    Those who unofficially support it by quelling opposition through intimidation or by subservient compliance?
- Who needs to feel the problem? How can they come to feel the problem?
- Who could provide opposition?
- Who could provide support?
    Those who currently support you?
    Those who don't yet support you but very likely would if asked?

     Those who like you personally?

     Those who would directly benefit from the changes sought?

     Those who because of philosophy or previous activism would like to be involved?

- Who has dealt with this type of issue before?

     Those in your own group?

     Those outside your immediate group (for example, experts)?

- Whom do you need to make sure that you don't leave out?
- Who will be pleased by your actions? Why?
- Who will be upset by your actions? Why?
- How will you deal with these reactions to strengthen your efforts?

In the very beginning you will have an answer to only a few of these questions. The most critical ones at this point relate to identifying others who can help you get things going. They, along with other people who will become involved, will be able to help provide some additional answers.

Change occurs through the responses of people. Knowing who the people are will enable you to target your efforts purposefully to promote the responses that help your community achieve its goals. You will have a better idea of what to anticipate and what to do.

Four: Begin to Involve Other People

As you grow in your understanding of the issue and of the people who are in some way or another affected, you begin to involve other people in the process. Start with those likely to be interested in the issue whom you know the best. Their personal relationship with you at this point is probably more important than their perceived relationship to the issue. Besides, it is easier to talk with people you know.

In the early stages of the enterprise you are asking people to help you figure out what can be done and to help you do it. Later, when your growing group has had some experience, you may very well invite people's participation by asking them to assist with a specific task.

Your initial conversations are more about the issue and the contemplation of action than they are about any particular action. That discussion must come soon, but first you must arouse a sense of interest that is sufficient for action. Even later, when you recruit new participants, it is the combination of the relationship of people to each other and their heightened interest in the issue that precedes the willingness to actually work for change.

This is actually a fairly quick process because you probably have a pretty good idea of who will want to do something. You may have a couple of conversations about the matter before you ask for some sort of commitment. Once you think the interest is there, you may very well ask point blank: "Do you want to do anything about this?" To the probable reply of "What do you want me to do?" your best answer is something like, "I'm not sure. We'll need to figure that out." (Again, when you are involving people past this very beginning stage, you will have some specific answers to that question.)

The next question to ask is, "Who else should we be talking to?" Together you determine other potential allies and decide who should talk to whom. Your initial conversations serve both to educate people as much as you can about the issue and to raise discomfort with the present situation. Your purpose is to create a readiness for action, even if it is some fairly simple action. At the conclusion of every conversation revisit this one question: "Who else should we be talking to?" On occasion you will want to work in pairs, creating new pairs as you go along. Pair a more experienced partner with a less experienced one. In this way you don't end up having only two or three people who are confident enough to recruit new members.

You talk with people, your partners talk with people, and pretty soon you have enough people to begin making some decisions about actions to take. You need only a handful of people to begin the discussion of what "doing something about this" might look like. This small group then moves you into the next phase of developing the beginnings of a more planful, organized approach to changing the situation.

Key Questions for Beginning to Involve Other People
- Whom do you know that you could talk to about this?
- What do you need to tell them to get them interested?
- How will you respond to their questions?
- What will you do if someone you counted on isn't willing to do anything?
- Who else should we be talking to?

Five: Figure Out What to Do

You progress to this phase of the effort in one of two ways. The first and most common way is to have a small group of people gather together to talk about and decide how your group should approach things. A second approach involves you or your small group stirring up a larger group that then gathers to make some decisions. In this case a smaller group still does need to spend time organizing the initial gathering to make sure the discussion moves past complaining and toward decisions for action. Regardless of your approach, the group that gathers talks about the matters that brought you together, what you want to accomplish, and where your starting point should be.

Throughout the life of your organized effort you will recognize that you use actions to bring attention and people to your effort and to get them involved in a meaningful way. The best way to enlist people is through action. You recruit to the action itself, to the issue the action is about, and to the group that is taking the action.

Very early on you will decide on a fairly simple, time-specific action that can be accomplished quickly—that is, in a matter of weeks, not months. It is difficult for many groups to move to the action phase. They spend meeting after meeting talking about things to do or getting ready to get ready to do something. This is usually because the perceived risk of failure is high, and it is compounded by trying to tackle something complex before you have much of a history of working with each other. To avoid this contrived hemming and hawing, focus on a short-term issue and select some immediate action.

This will get you going. Initial, immediate actions have some other benefits as well. You will capitalize on existing interest and excite new interest. You will draw attention to your group and your issue. You will be able to make a noticeable gain. Your willingness to take action and your early success will build confidence. You can use this action to test and develop the leadership of more than one individual. You will quickly learn who is more interested in talk and whom you can count on to actually do things. One additional benefit is that you confirm the action orientation of your group. You promote group norms relating to action rather than to talking about the problem.

The best short-term actions merely require people to show up with a general idea of what to do when they get there. It is very important though to have someone *prepared* who can *clearly* show them what to do when they get there. If there is some sort of festive atmosphere, all the better. Be sure that what you are asking people to do is something they can see themselves doing. Actions of this sort might include painting a graffiti covered wall, planting trees, standing at a major intersection holding signs, or packing an agency board meeting. Actions that don't put people's knowledge of the issue to the test or that don't require them to convince strangers of anything are the easiest.

There is a delicate balance between taking an immediate action and acting without a clear sense of the overall direction of the effort. You have to think about how big or far-reaching a plan you need to make. You have to decide for yourself how immediate your focus can be without getting in your own way. If you don't look far enough ahead, you can make things more difficult for yourselves down the road by what you do today. (I hasten to add that you will also very probably make things more difficult for yourselves down the road by doing nothing today.) You also don't want to be caught up in just moving from one specific action to the next without organizing your actions to make real, discernable progress.

It's kind of like walking down the street. You can't look only at where you are planting each step or you might get lost—that is, if you don't run into something. You also can't keep your gaze forever locked on the horizon or you are likely to step in a hole or on something that you wished you hadn't.

A good alternative in the beginning is to create an initial action that clearly relates to your issue, then follow that success with more substantive planning. You need to do some more thorough planning as soon as you are ready, but not before. Detailed planning too often serves as a substitute for action, not a preparation for it.

In any type of planning, you are going from general notions to specific actions. Regardless of how far down the road you look, answering some basic questions can help you figure out what you need to do.

Key Questions for Figuring Out What to Do
- What outcomes do you want to produce? What does "better" look like?
- Which actions or solutions might help your group achieve that?
- What activity or particular thing are you going to focus on? What does your group want to *start* with?
- What does your group need to take care of? What are the main pieces of the activity? What have you put in place to be sure these things are dealt with?

Before you take on the next questions, it is time to appoint the Nag. The Nag records everyone's commitments and summarizes them at the end of the meeting to see that they are accurate. The Nag then calls each person a few days *before* the commitment is to be completed. The Nag is a role the group agrees to have filled, and the person is selected by the group. This person's job is so important that this is about the only work he or she does for the organization. Now on to the next questions.

- What specific steps are you going to take?
- When will you take them?
- Who will do them? How will you spread the work around?
- How will you know that these things got done?

By this time you have decided to act. You have a better understanding of the issue. You know more about the people affected. You have actually gotten a few folks to join you. You have even planned an action you can take to get things going. How long did all this take? It need not take very long at all.

The time-distance between Step One and Step Five can be traveled fairly quickly when you are just getting started. It can be completed within a week, at the most a month. The time it takes to accomplish these steps the first time through depends more on people's schedules than on the quantity of work that needs to be performed. At this point in the process things are not very complex, but you have quickly come a long way from just worrying about things.

Now you are in a position to do what this is all about. You are poised to take action.

Six: Take Action

Of course, none of the previous five steps means anything unless and until you take the sixth step. Feeling offended by improper conditions may confirm your moral righteousness. Wanting things to be different shows that you care a bit about what is happening. Acting to make things different is what ultimately counts.

As we have discussed (OK, so we haven't really discussed it, you and I, but you have read about it), your initial action should be a fairly small, concrete activity designed to make progress by putting ideas into operation while drawing supporters and attention to your cause.

All right, you have figured out some specific thing to do, and in this step you do it. In actual practice an action really is the culmination of a series of actions, which put all the necessary pieces into place. So it is critical that you follow up and follow through on all assignments leading up to the action itself. There is a radical difference between trying to do something and completing it (as in "I tried to call him, but he wasn't in"). You are going to have holes if all the pieces haven't been completed. The more holes you have, the more likely that your action will fall through.

Do what needs to be done to make your action work. A good idea is to do the simple things right away. There is nothing like ticking a few things off your "to do" list to make you think you are doing something. You feel that things are starting to move and that the endeavor is becoming real.

When you are engaged in the action itself, it is important to keep the intended outcomes of the action clearly in focus. Getting the activity started is an important step, but that is not enough. You are not through until the activity is through. (You will learn the rule of the final inch shortly.) Pay close attention during the activity so you can prompt here or nudge there when necessary to accomplish its purpose. I would offer a caution on the side of gentleness and poise. Avoid acting overstressed or pushy, otherwise you will undermine the confidence and spirit of your crew. Remember, those are important outcomes as well.

Key Questions for Taking Action
- Has the groundwork for the action been properly laid, and has your group completed preparations?
- Do you have someone to direct and manage the action who is prepared to do so in an encouraging way?
- Are participants enjoying what they are doing?
- Are people recognizing the fact that they are taking real action and contributing to making things better?
- Are you using this action to build enthusiasm and commitment?
- Are you attracting the attention you want?
- Are you accomplishing the other purposes that you expected?

Seven: Use the Action

The action itself will make things different, simply because you have introduced something new into the immediate environment. Thus, everything changes. It is like throwing a stone into a body of water. It creates ripples. The larger the stone and the smaller the body of water, the more significant those ripples will be. But there will be ripples in all cases. Beyond anything else you bring about, the activity itself will have an effect. You can increase that effect, however, by the things you do around the activity.

The action has value to you before, during, and after the time it actually takes place. The more you recognize and use its potential, the greater benefit you will derive from it. These benefits occur primarily in three areas. First, the action can teach you. Second, the action can build your organization. Third, the action can produce a change in conditions.

The action can help you learn more about the issue as you prepare yourself to educate participants and others who may witness the action. As you educate, you will learn. You will also develop a heightened sense of attentiveness so that you begin to notice little bits of information or reactions from particular people that give you added insight into the matter itself.

You will learn more about the target of your efforts, those whose behavior you are trying to change. You are becoming more aware of the things the target responds to and how it responds. You begin to see what the target is prepared to do or not do, and you will get at least an inkling of how the target is preparing for future actions, either theirs or yours.

You can use the action to learn more about the members of your organization. You get a better idea of what they are willing and able to do at this point, and what they will need to be willing and able to do more. You are starting to see how people work together, and you are spotting potential areas of conflict that you can address before problems get big. You are discovering potential leaders.

By acting and preparing to act, you are learning more about what you are doing. You better understand what works, what doesn't, and what needs fine tuning. You are learning about other resources you need, and you are beginning to get ideas on how to get them.

Your action helps develop the organization. All of you are gaining more experience, and with experience comes more confidence. All the things you are learning will make your future efforts more effective.

Your action provides recruitment opportunities. Preparation for the event gives you something specific to involve people in, and the action itself can attract new people to your organization. The attention generated by the activity can let a portion of the community know you exist and that you are real. They become more aware of the issue and your commitment to do something about it.

The members of your organization feel better about themselves simply because they are doing something. It feels good to act, not just talk, and it feels good to produce. You increase motivation and commitment when you help participants recognize anything they have accomplished by the action. The recognition of progress begets an interest in more progress.

The action will diminish the three major barriers of fear, apathy, and ignorance.

Certainly the action brings change. You have set things in motion. Once things are in motion, you can keep things moving and accelerate the pace of change. Even a small, initial action can help get things unstuck.

Key Questions for Using the Action
- What are you learning?
- What should you do differently the next time? What should you do the same?

- Who seems to have leadership abilities?
- What other things do you need, and how can you get them?
- How are you using this action to bring in new members and to give them something to do?
- Who noticed what you did?
- How can you capitalize on the responses you are getting?
    From the public?
    From the target?
    From your members?
- How can you keep things going?

Eight: Repeat the Steps You Have Taken

Now you are ready to move on to more significant activities and other, perhaps somewhat more challenging, issues. Keep things going, most especially in the early stages, or the forces of the status quo will fairly quickly nudge things back to their old order.

Every subsequent action begins with a decision to act. Now your understanding of the issue and your analysis of the situation, particularly the actors in the play, needs to deepen. You will create more opportunities for involving people, and you will figure out more things to do. You will do more things and use the benefits those actions will bring. You will repeat the cycle anew. As you do, you will become more capable, more visible, and more powerful.

As you move forward, the organization that is beginning to develop will need some attention. Some outline of structure will be needed. That structure should emerge from the needs of the organization as it is acting rather than being imposed on it.

Any structure you decide on ought to be flexible, and it should help the organization work more easily and more effectively. Structure that gets in the way of what the organization is trying to do will frustrate rather than facilitate. In a change effort primarily given life by people who could be doing other things with their time, this self-created frustration can be deadly. You may need to remind yourself that structure is supposed to serve the work of the organization; the work of the organization is not supposed to serve the structure.

Effectively structuring your work will reduce tension, reduce wasted energy, and increase productivity. Fairly early on, you will begin to determine things such as how decisions are made and how communication among members is to occur. You will develop ways to more effectively determine what work needs to be done and how it can be organized. You may need to figure out how you will handle money and other resources that may be given to the effort. You will find ways to keep an overall sense of direction. Again, bring your structure along naturally, allowing it to grow out of what you are doing, and take a look from time to time to see that your procedures are helping rather than getting in the way.

Once you have become fairly active, these eight steps will seem to blur, some occurring simultaneously with others. This is natural and appropriate. To remain effective, however, you must consciously attend to the Essential Eight to make sure that no aspect of the process is being taken for granted.

Every sequence of actions brings a chapter to a close and allows a new set of opportunities to unfold. The preliminary activities you engaged in the first time through these steps have begun making things different. These activities have established that you are real and intending to act with purpose. It is likely that you began with a fairly small group of interested souls. You now have discovered that you do not need a lot of people to get started, though you may need a lot of people ultimately to succeed. Your actions the first time through or the second or the sixteenth will bring in more people, more other resources, and more recognition from the community.

Planned, organized change is a process of building until you have changed the climate sufficiently and built enough power and tackled enough issues that you have truly changed how things occur and will occur in your community.

Key Questions for Repeating the Steps You Have Taken

- Are you willing to do something about this?
- What more do you need to know about the issue?
- What are you learning about the actors in the play?
- How are you developing leadership?
- How do you keep necessary people informed? Who are those necessary people?
- How do you keep people connected to each other?
- How are you going to make decisions?
- What are your next steps?
- Who will take them?
- Are you still taking action?
- What are you learning?

Twenty Tips for Taking Action

Think ahead.   What do you need to do to make sure the things you are doing will work? The organization's efforts will make things different. You are getting reactions from people. How will you respond to those changed conditions? Anticipate. Prepare.

Keep it interesting.   People stay with people and things they enjoy.

Identify necessary time frames.   To accomplish what you want to accomplish, what needs to be done when? What's the date for "done on time"? If something is to be done by a certain date, when does it need to be started? You can't do everything at once, and you don't have to.

Notice and communicate progress.   Keep people aware that they have come a way, maybe a long way, from where they started. Recognition of progress cannot be assumed.

Keep in communication.   Communication is what connects people to each other, to the issue, and to the work of the organization. Communication makes things real and worthy of the emotional and time investments required for organized action. Unconnected people are invisible people.

Distribute the work and the glory.   Everybody matters, and everybody has something to contribute. Contributions of time and talent lead to greater levels of commitment. Intentionally seek those contributions, and recognize efforts publicly and privately. If only a few people are seen as important, the others will be seen and see themselves as unimportant. What could be the consequences of that?

Develop leadership.   You can do nothing more important to develop the organization than to develop leadership. Create opportunities. Make invitations. Encourage and nurture.

Recruit, recruit, recruit.   Your organization will never have too many people, and it will always be losing a few. You need to both build and replenish. The most critical source of resources and subsequent power are the people you have involved in the effort. Although the issue and action of the organization will attract some people, you cannot rely on these alone. You must actively recruit. Always.

Promote learning and do your homework.   Learn from everything that happens and everything you do. Seek out information that you do not have. You need to know more about the issue, the people affected by it, the actions you need to take, and the strengths and weaknesses of your organization. Don't be the only one in your organization who is committed to learning.

Keep hope alive.   Hope drives action. People will act only if they believe in the possibility of a successful outcome from their actions.

Maintain the tension between dissatisfaction and attraction.   The more that people are dissatisfied with current conditions or attracted by alternative conditions, the more likely they are to work to produce alternative conditions. Fan the flames of dissatisfaction and spur excitement over new possibilities. Complacent and apathetic people watch TV.

Take only the actions you are capable of taking.   Don't pretend. Don't discourage members by creating conditions for frustration and failure. Do build capability.

Keep people and tasks organized.   Know how tasks are related to the goal and to other tasks. Understand how tasks can be broken down into smaller pieces, and know what those pieces are. Do participants know what they are supposed to do, how to do it, and why this is important to the overall effort? How do you know if things are getting done?

Keep your effort visible.   Get the attention you need from the broader community, from potential supporters, and from the target. What is the attention you need?

Stay on top of the situation.   Follow up and follow through. You don't need to know what every single person is doing, but do keep informed about the actions that are being taken.

Create a range of opportunities for involvement.   People have different interests and different degrees of available time. Opportunities can range from very small and occasional to persistent and significant. Make sure that planning and action preparation and leadership opportunities remain available. Can you answer the question "What can I do?" regardless of who asks it?

If you are not getting the involvement from others that you want or you are not maintaining that involvement, *you* need to do things differently. Complaining will not solve the problem. Only acting differently will.

Act ethically.   Reflect on your inactions as well as your actions. Your ethics are not to be used as excuses for inaction, nor are they to be ignored for the sake of convenience. They both direct and give meaning to your actions. Use them as fundamental guides.

Be prepared for tactics others will use on you.   You are not the only people who are acting to protect or assert their perceived interests. What are other folks up to?

Deal only with those who can make decisions.   When it is time for decisions to be made, direct communication between decision makers is necessary. Unequal patterns of power are confirmed when only one party's decision maker is actively involved in the discussions. Representatives carry messages and filter them. You can carry your own messages, and you don't need a filter.

Make those who need to feel the problem actually feel it.   People who are happy with the current situation will not act to change it. Those who maintain the problem must come to feel sufficiently uncomfortable with trying to keep the problem before they will move toward change. Who needs to feel the problem? How can they come to feel it?

Using the Essential Eight along with the Rules of the Game (presented in Part II) will help you accomplish so much more with your community than so many others who act on good intentions alone. You honor your community and you honor yourself when you decide to take part in giving strength and purpose to hope. Now let's take a look at those rules.

The Rules of the Game

CHAPTER 3

Basic Things to Know

T he field of community change can seem daunting, especially when you first enter it, although you will quickly become more confident and ambitious once you gain some experience with the conditions within which change occurs. You will come to know its rhythms and expect its vagaries. If you have already been involved in a number of change efforts, you know that even seasoned change agents can get lost when they begin to take things for granted. This set of rules, the basic things you need to know, will introduce you to the fundamental principles that govern effective change efforts. These principles will help make the territory a little more recognizable once you start walking around in it, and they will remind you of key features to help you keep your bearings.

The rules in this chapter form the foundation of your understanding. They are less about what you should do and more about what you should know to guide what you do. Underlying the Rules of the Game are some important recurring themes of successful change efforts that are listed below. If you have been involved in other change efforts, these themes may seem like old friends. If this is your first change effort, revisit these themes often. They will help you keep your feet firmly planted on the road to successful change.

Promoting change is about human relations, human actions, and human reactions. Your group's ability to effectively manage your relationships with one another and with your allies and opponents is fundamental to the strength of the effort and the development of strategies and tactics. The rules will help you take a look at the potential for stress among these relationships and the opportunities for strength. Understanding what aids or interferes with action and knowing what kinds of reactions you can anticipate are essential to successful action.

Promoting change requires organized efforts. You will need to bring together a number of people who can learn to act powerfully and in concert. These people will provide the necessary credibility, perspectives, and resources to the cause. The more these elements are present and the more they are organized, the more likely you will succeed. The rules will help you examine the elements that strengthen your organization and identify factors that contribute to or get in the way of using your strengths.

The various levels of interest and involvement of participants in the effort must be recognized, legitimized, and assessed to help you understand your strengths, risks, and opportunities. Further, the work of positive community change is done mostly by people who are not paid to make this happen. The rules will help you appreciate the unique demands and opportunities this brings.

Promoting change challenges entrenched interests, routine expectations, and common behaviors. You are going to shake things up— maybe just a little, maybe a lot. Those who fear a loss from the impending change as well as those who might benefit from it will be disturbed out of the ordinary. You may well encounter resistance and even direct opposition. The rules will help you to better understand the various types and sources of resistance and provide you with some ways for handling it.

Promoting change requires power. Action contributes to empowerment. Building the organization contributes to empowerment. And empowerment, in turn, strengthens the action and the organization. Power, its development and use, can be a difficult subject. The rules offer a broad view of power that goes well beyond the idea of power as dominance. Power is not dominance, but it can be used to dominate. It certainly should be used thoughtfully and purposefully. That it must be used is certain.

Promoting change involves encountering a range of obstacles. It is often the unseen, rather than the apparent, obstacles that undermine change efforts. The rules will help you to better understand the nature of these stumbling blocks. You then can avoid some of them and deal effectively with the others.

Promoting change requires a sense of optimism. In the beginning of most efforts, optimism will probably be in short supply. After all, if there were already plenty available, people would already have acted to improve things. But there is always some optimism, and it grows. It grows when you connect one person's bit of optimism with another, and then another. It grows when you link it to signs of success. The rules will help you see the importance of this source of energy and how you can help it grow.

Promoting change involves engaging uncertainty and embracing the unknown.   Promoting change involves shaping the future, which will be shaped by countless forces, only a few of which you hold in your hands. Going from the known to the unknown is difficult. You will see this acted out in many ways. The rules acknowledge that people promoting change will need to act in different, nonroutine ways so that other people begin to act differently.

Promoting change requires that you move past pretending or denying what you are likely to face.   Have no false hopes, but do have some very real ones. Make sure that you place your hopes on the things you can count on. The rules offer encouragement and caution and give you a clearer sense of what you can expect.

Promoting change is a process.   Successful change depends on a series of decisions by those who have sufficient power to create something new. Especially early on, these decisions will be questioned—maybe even actively resisted. Support for change must extend beyond the early implementation phase, allowing it to become sufficiently rooted to draw the sustenance it needs. The rules acknowledge the importance of nurturing the process, giving it the strength it needs to sustain itself.

You will trace these themes through your awareness that the process of change affects the interests of people, who in turn affect the process of change. You will see how these themes become entangled with your frustrations. You will recognize their presence in issues of power, and you will use these themes to strengthen your own change efforts.

After all this, change is quite possible. In fact, change will happen—whether or not you do anything about it. Your work will help accelerate the nature and direction of that change to benefit the people and things you care about. You could rely on the people who are used to getting their way to shape the future without your participation. Sometimes their interests and yours are the same. Sometimes not. Your decision to become part of the process of change, your decision to learn how to do that more effectively, at the very least suggests that the people and things you care about do matter.

As you undertake an interest in promoting organized change for the first time or the fortieth, you will discover that knowledge of these fundamental themes will guide you, directing you to see beneath the surface to recognize what is occurring, what is likely to occur, and what needs to occur. Your ability to make decisions and to act effectively will be built on these insights.

No road map can tell you everything you will encounter on your journey. Neither will the following rules. Each situation you face will be similar to others, and each will have some new discoveries to offer. Understanding the Rules of the Game will help you determine what to look out for and how to proceed when you make the decision to help strengthen a community. You will have a little more confidence because you have a better idea of where you are going and some idea of how to get there.

Acting to Change People's Interests

The process of change affects the interests of people and is affected by the actions of people who participate in the process. Change is a process of introducing new actions to provoke new reactions. All this acting and reacting is done by people to protect or assert their interests. This provides the dynamic context in which change occurs. This set of rules introduces you to some fundamental factors that influence involvement in change.

Those who play the game make the rules

The house in which I grew up was graced by a big backyard. It was where we neighborhood kids played baseball. Whoever designed this expanse apparently did not have a baseball field in mind, but we adapted. We ran into other difficulties as well. There was some variety of age and quite a variety of talent among the would-be ballplayers who showed up to play.

These quirks of design and ability led to a Catalina Street redefinition of the grand game. If you were of a certain age, you had to bat left-handed. (The older ones were all righties.) But in so doing, you could bring the kitchen windows into play. Breaking a window meant the end of the inning for the team at bat. (There were other, less important rules about fixing the window later.) A ball hit over the fence was both a home run and an out. (Mr. Kirby would yell at us if he saw us climbing his fence, and so would my folks—and Mr. Kirby had two dogs.) So it went. We made up the rules to serve our purposes.

Every now and then visiting adults would watch us for a few innings and, being adults, tell us how the game should be played. Often this had to do with giving more breaks to the younger kids or the less skilled players. This caused some consternation for us who were "serious" about the game. They really didn't understand what this was all about. New kids had the same problem. They'd get mad when they discovered that one of our backyard regulations meant that the run didn't count and they had to go back to third. But it all worked for us regulars. (By the way, the rule about batting left-handed was introduced by a couple of us who could switch-hit pretty well.)

On a more sobering note, I have asked more than 4,000 social work or human services students to name their state senator and two state representatives or assembly members (the system most states have for their legislature). I have had six students answer this question correctly. Six. Not a good proportion.

Whether it's baseball in the backyard or new wisdom coming from Phoenix, Sacramento, Hartford, or Washington DC, those involved in the game design rules that work for them. Sometimes this includes trying to keep others from getting into the game. Whether it is legislative politics, agency politics, neighborhood politics, or family politics, it is highly unlikely that those who develop the rules do so in a way that results in a loss to themselves. Far more common are policies designed to protect the interests of those involved in making the decisions.

The fewer people participating in the decision-making process, the more narrow the protected interests are likely to be. In actual practice, those who don't participate just don't count. Take advantage of your rights to participate in shaping policies, regulations, and norms that affect you and the people you care about. If these rights are not readily open to you, demand them. If you stand back and allow others to make the rules, be ready to accept the consequences.

It's not "them"

I often ask community groups to describe a community problem that affects the members of the group. I then ask: "Whose behavior has to change to make things better? Who needs to start acting differently?" The answer, in one way or another, almost always comes back: "THEM." It sure as heck ain't "US." Right?

After a pause, another question: "And just how do you expect THEM to change if all of US keep doing the same things?" Sorry, the answer "Well, they just should!" doesn't cut it. Short of miraculous conversion, the "thems" are just going to keep doing what they have been doing all along until something or someone comes along to get them to do something different.

This rule is somewhat an extension of the previous one. It speaks to the necessity of taking part in processes to alter circumstances that you (we) don't like. This does not mean that you have to or can be responsible for the actions of others. It does mean that you have to take responsibility for your own actions in situations that you find unacceptable. Whether or not we like it, "them" is likely to be part of "us." Members of a community are connected in some way. The actions of one group affect the consequences felt by others. The potential for both partnership and internal competition exists.

Imagine you and someone else sitting at opposite ends of a teeter-totter. If one of you introduces a change to the equation, the other person's position will change. You push up, they go down. You move to the end and get a couple of your friends to hang on too, and the other is stuck high in the air. Can't avoid it. Your behavior contributes to, maintains, or changes circumstances. Which will it be? The only way we can expect "them" to behave differently is if "we" behave differently.

People are the allies and the targets

All this business about community change—the strategies, the tactics, the planning, the forces at play, all of it—is just about people and what they do. I mention this here before we go much further because, obvious as it may seem, it's just as easy to forget.

The people, those who are on your side, those opposing you, or those unaware of your struggles, are petty and brave, peevish and principled. They can sacrifice and show themselves noble. And they will remind you that we are important to one another.

I have seen activists treat the people working in their organizations as pets. I have seen them build opponents into giants. I have amazed myself by half expecting those who have a stake in things to act in some way different from regular people. It has been a surprise to me that I have been surprised when the ordinary happens.

People will generally operate within a range that is known, and this includes behavior that might at first seem odd. Understanding that people respond to their perception of their circumstances, not just yours, will help you make sense of things and will diminish your frustration. Taking this understanding into account as you analyze the situation (which, after all, is just people acting—or not) will help you know what to expect and how to relate.

When stripped of our titles, labels, and positions in the social order, we are all equally important. Removed from identification with a particular cause, institution, company, or other construct of human fabrication, people are just doing what they can to make their way to what they think is important. Recognizing this will help you to see things a little more clearly and to figure out what to do as you, yourself, make your own way.

One final note. Remembering that people are the allies and the targets means that you have to think about how you will treat them. Aside from tactical considerations, there are moral ones. Precisely what this means to you will be informed by your own moral code. Just make sure you bring it along.

Any problem that involves more than just you will require more than just you to resolve it

You can't do it alone. Don't try. Of course, being the lone crusader does have its emotional benefits. You can see yourself as courageous. You can see yourself as action-oriented. You can even see yourself as superior to all those sluggards who haven't moved to action. You just may not be able to see yourself as successful in producing a meaningful change. You decide what's important.

Frankly, to my way of thinking, being ineffective is not noble. Assuming that you can single-handedly represent the views and concerns of others borders on arrogance. You need the perspectives and resources of others, including the added power their involvement brings to the situation.

Certainly, you can be a powerful force to push the process forward, to motivate and lead. This is important and valuable. But in doing so, develop the capabilities of others as well. The more people you have acting capably, the easier things are going to be.

Too often the initiators of change act in ways that dismiss or undermine the capabilities of potential allies and partners, almost as if they don't really see or believe in the value of the contributions others can make. Too frequently change agents limit the number of people who are seen as important. One has to wonder what the real goals are. These errors can lead to the change agent standing pretty much alone complaining that "nobody really cares." What do you think is really going on?

Effective change agents understand that encouraging and developing the participation of others requires skill and purpose. Many things can get in the way of people becoming involved:

- Not knowing that they are needed
- Not knowing how they can help
- Feeling inadequate for the tasks at hand
- Fear of reprisal
- Fear of failure
- Being shut out of decision making
- Even the barrier of never before having considered that they can make a difference

Effective change agents know that these and other obstacles to involvement are normal and can be dealt with. They know that they can't do it alone, so they figure out how to do it together.

Remember, whenever I refer to "you," I am not referring to you as a change agent working alone but rather to all the people who are acting with you to promote the change.

You don't have to involve everybody

Hmm . . . doesn't this contradict that whole business of involving people? No. Although you do need to continue to expand the number of people engaged in the effort, you cannot and need not really involve everyone.

Unless the group affected by the change is very small, you need the active involvement of only a small percentage of the community to produce the change. This small, active group can mobilize others when necessary. Also, understand that there will be a number of different levels of participation. Some people will be part of the core leadership group, others will contribute by helping out when asked, still others may show up just on occasion or for some fairly specific activity. This is normal. Not everyone is going to have the same interest or commitment. It would be a mistake to count only the most highly involved as "real" contributors. You must be able to see all those who are currently involved as potentially significant contributors. The trick is to develop opportunities that encourage more participation and commitment for more people—without expecting that everyone has to act the same.

Turnover in leadership and membership is natural

Developing methods to involve more people is important because a number, maybe even a lot, of people will drift away over time. This is especially important when it comes to leadership. What the change effort needs in its early stages is different from what it will need at later stages. Some early leaders are not interested in or capable of providing for those later needs. So, some turnover is not only to be expected but may very well be healthy.

Unfortunately, the loss of some participants can lead to discouragement among those remaining. This can be true even if participation is generally growing. When you understand that some loss is natural and give adequate attention to development of new leadership and recruitment of new members, you will be able to take these changes in stride.

Human capital is the most valuable resource of any enterprise

Because other people offer the additional power, encouragement, information, talents, skills, energy, and anything else that is needed for a successful change effort, a wise change agent will create an organization that values its people. You need to understand and deal purposefully with the issues, but your issues and your approaches to the change effort fundamentally revolve around people.

There are many ways to deal with people that will demonstrate their inherent value to the organization. A full list can probably never be written. Given that, however, in my experience the following guidelines are fundamental to preserving and enhancing the human capital of your change effort.

Get to know one another. The more we know one another on a personal level, the more opportunity we have to discover connections we have with others. Maybe we find a couple of other people who like hockey, some who garden, another who grew up in Des Moines. These links provide additional dimensions to our relationships, which help us to enjoy one another's company and to weather some of the challenges that lie ahead. These more numerous strands in our relationships provide resiliency, a kind of safety net that strengthens our ability to handle the inevitable frustrations—some with one another—that will occur over the course of our work. They make the group more attractive and comfortable and increase a sense of being included. *A cohesive group is a strong group.*

Respect different interests and time availability. People will have different levels of interest in the issue and draw satisfaction from different activities as they pursue the issue. Use this awareness to help create meaningful roles for people in the organization. I am surprised at how rarely people are actually asked what they would like to do.

People's level and range of interest can grow if given the chance. Often this is a function of their confidence in understanding the organization, becoming familiar with other members, and in being able to display their lack of knowledge about some new type of activity.

We rarely expect people to give more money than they can give, but we often do imply that they should give more time. Giving time is, after all, a matter of both interest and availability. As interest grows, more time can be "found." Even those very interested have some real time constraints, however, and these should be accepted. A person who believes that her or his time constraints are appreciated will more willingly invest in the effort because it feels safe to do so.

Respect different points of view.   A spirit of inquiry and discovery will strengthen the organization. Examine a situation from various points of view; this will liberate thinking and promote support for the decisions the group reaches. Disagreement is based on better ideas (there is rarely one *best* idea) rather than right or wrong ideas, making it easier for the group to move ahead after having considered different views. When this is done as a matter of routine, the holder of a minority view is more likely to support the generally agreed-upon direction.

When diverse thinking is not encouraged, disagreements can become tests of wills with the loser harboring resentment. The resulting resistance may undermine the support for decisions necessary for action. Further, when nonconforming or apparently less valid ideas are summarily dismissed or even laughed at, not only does the person who offered the idea feel offended or embarrassed but others will attempt to prevent that from happening to them by simply deciding not to offer their own opinions. Commitment and valuable insights are lost in the process.

Respecting different points of view includes valuing cultural diversity. Different cultural groups will have different perspectives, different experiences, and different norms relating to the issues the group is working on. Diversity provides variety, giving the entire organization rich sources of understanding and direction.

Differences offer the group the potential for conflict among its members or an opportunity for strength. Differences will exist. It would be a mistake to pretend and act otherwise. Legitimizing and utilizing diversity will strengthen the group as long as doing so is genuinely directed toward accomplishing a shared goal.

Recognize contributions and let people know they are valued.   You cannot assume people know that their work and their presence is appreciated. None of us likes to feel that we are being taken for granted. Members of the organization should make a point of noting the contributions of one another. This is not something only those in leadership positions should do.

The methods for expressing appreciation can be simple or conspicuous. A simple comment, genuinely made, may be more meaningful than a plaque. Recognition for a specific act or set of actions makes more of an impact than one that is of a more general nature.

Giving attention to members' participation and specific contributions fosters a climate of acceptance and worth—two very important matters for us social beings.

Keep people informed.   Members of the organization need to know what is going on. From the very beginning this is important. The more that members know, the more they can contribute to the effort. Of the many things members should know, a particular set stands out as especially important:

- The issue or issues being addressed by the organization
- The nature of the organization and how it works
- Members' responsibilities (what to do and how to do it) and how that contributes to the success of the effort
- Opportunities for leadership

Further, members should be kept apprised of the progress of the organization, particularly the gains being made and the challenges the group is facing. This can be done simply and routinely. I'm not talking about making people sign up for a class here.

If members aren't kept informed, they become confined to a very limited role, their enthusiasm will likely wane, and their potential for leadership will be stunted. Neglecting to keep people informed conveys a subtle notion that only certain members of the organization really need, want, or can properly handle information. This tends to imply that some members of the group are more important or valued than others. Further, the more fragmented the view of the situation, the more likely it will be inaccurate. Individuals may make up details; in fact, they have to if they do not have sufficient and timely information. This may influence not only their actions but also how they represent the organization.

Being well-grounded in the issues builds both confidence and commitment. This is also true for understanding how the organization works. Think about how hard it is to become enthused about something you really know little about. It's hard to figure out what to do, much less why you should do it. You feel a little awkward trying to explain it to others, and you really hope they won't ask. In contrast, when you feel somewhat knowledgeable about an issue or an activity, you not only answer questions but find ways to bring it up in conversation. Whether it is the World Wide Web, teachings from the Koran, or golf, you feel more equipped to engage in both discussion and action.

Again, members need to be informed of progress. This sustains and encourages their participation.

Deal with people directly.   The more that people are in direct contact with one another, the more a sense of partnership is cultivated. This is particularly true when it involves matters of disagreement or conflict. Finding out second- or third-hand that someone is saying something uncomplimentary about you behind your back destroys trust. Don't do that to others. If you are having difficulty with another member, speak directly to that individual, not about what they are or are not doing but about what you are perceiving and how that affects you. Give the individual an opportunity to correct your perceptions or to make changes. For this to work you have to be genuinely open to both possibilities—as well as being open to making some changes of your own.

Much of the time internal conflict occurs as a result of differences in expectations about what someone is supposed to do or not do. When differences start becoming apparent, address them in a straightforward, down-to-earth manner. By the way, these usually are just that—differences. Rarely are they matters of right and wrong or good and bad. Handle them accordingly.

The way members of a group manage internal disappointments or disagreements is a critical variable leading to success or failure. In my experience, most groups fall apart not because the external challenges are too great but because the internal challenges prove too difficult. The way you conduct yourself in these situations will help set the tone for the group as a whole.

Develop abilities, confidence, and leadership.   As a general rule, be on the lookout for opportunities to strengthen these elements. Whenever possible, ask yourself how any action of the organization lends itself to members' growth. Helping members understand how to do their tasks and what these activities mean to the success of the effort signals that they and what they do matters. If, at the same time, members recognize that they can increase their responsibilities and help set direction for the operation, their sense of affiliation is firmed.

Too often members are closed off from leadership roles or other important actions because those in charge don't think others really know enough to perform these roles effectively. Not only does this lead to very narrow leadership and weak investment in action by others, but it also contributes to a few people ending up doing most of the work. It is essential to find ways for members to grow in their abilities, confidence, and leadership potential.

Each group needs a mainstay, someone who provides continuous assurance to other members

The clock says the meeting has begun. Everybody's casting quick, anxious glances at everybody else. Someone's not here. Without anyone saying anything, you know this is true. A murmur of fuzzy, half-felt conversation takes the place of anything more meaningful until "she" arrives. Fairly competent people shift in their seats acting lost, wandering around the minutes as if they have never been here before. "She" doesn't have any particular title, no official position in the group, but her absence is as compelling as her presence. If this person never shows up, most decisions are stamped "tentative." That's if the group decides anything at all beyond "there's probably not enough of us here, we should probably reschedule."

All right. Maybe this depiction is a bit overdrawn, but I have witnessed this scene played out in various forms many times.

Each group seems to need a few people who serve as the providers of assurance. Most change efforts involve activities that are not a routine part of what people do every day. Most participants are volunteers who require some orientation and reorientation. Naturally there is a little uncertainty, which is relieved by working with someone who seems to know what she or he is doing. It's as much "tell us we can do" as it is "tell us what to do." The newer the group is, the more important this need seems to be.

The sad fact is that the person who can offer that much needed energy and confidence may well both love and hate the role and the expectations that flow from it. This "leader" may feel burdened and irritated at others for not assuming more responsibility for energizing and directing the organization. At the same time, he or she may like the feeling of importance that comes from being so critical to the success of the group. The trick is to increase the number of people who can fill this role. (By the way, a mainstay need not be noisy or showy.)

The group can move toward more shared confidence when members get into the habit of asking each other for opinions and then acting on those opinions. The process for identifying mainstays is expedited by creating several visible roles of responsibility within the organization. These provide opportunities for a number of members to be tested. Some will come to be seen as people who can be relied on to provide leadership. People need to have a chance to shine before they have confidence in themselves and others have confidence in them.

Then there is the important matter of approval. If all ideas need to meet the approval of one or two people, the group cannot act unless those one or two people are present. However, if even the more visible leaders ask for approval both from the group in general and on occasion from some particular people who are potential leaders, the responsibility for decisions and actions shifts to more shoulders. Members gain confidence by seeing a number of strong, capable people whenever they get together.

If this role falls to you, recognize both its value and the importance of grooming others who can give the group a sense of capability.

Everything happens through relationships

Coming together in the first place generally requires some sort of invitation offered and accepted between parties who know each other sufficiently well to perform that ritual. It's one person knowing another at least a little that get things rolling in the first place, and it's more people getting to know more people better that will keep it rolling.

Damn, it was frustrating. They had all been playing together for a couple of years. I hadn't been on the team long enough to know everyone's name, and most didn't know mine. On the rare occasions when I got the ball, I was expected to pass, not even dribble, just pass. I couldn't believe it, on any other team I'd always racked up the points. Of course, here, no one knew that, or acted like they cared to. I was out of sync, out of rhythm. I couldn't seem to get going.

Where have you been an outsider? How did that affect how you acted? Where have you kept people at arm's length? How much did you receive from them?

For people to work together well, some degree of trust must exist between them, and that trust must be as strong as the issues it supports are important to the parties involved. Sometimes, as in the case of opponents who finally agree to a common course of action, that trust may be placed outside a relationship, such as in a contract. The more firmly that trust is rooted in the relationship itself, however, the more willing the parties will be to offer and receive one another's assets.

We are more ready to invest in the known than the unknown. The more we know and feel we understand other parties, the more confident we are in our ability to determine how much we will rely on them. This seems to be a sort of dance. People get to know each other, and the give and take of a working relationship grows. When they know each other better, the range of mutually acceptable working behaviors expands. The relationship reaches its limits or hits a snag, and reliance on each other correspondingly stalls or retracts. If obstacles can be overcome, confidence, however tentative, begins to grow again.

You feel this. That little touch of confidence on seeing a familiar face. That twinge of hesitance in phoning an unfamiliar name. Things are easier with those you know.

Meetings begin with apparently nonproductive small talk before the order "Let's get down to business" is declared. The fact is that the group has already been down to business. Granted, this is business of a different sort. This is the business of reminding us who we are with each other, how we know each other, and testing to see if anything about this might change.

This does not mean that everyone in the change effort must become your new best friend, although you and anyone else probably won't work very long with people you don't like if you don't have to. It does mean that feeling comfortable with each other as we relate to the purpose of the organization makes it easier for us to get things done. Effective relationships make possible the recognition of complementary talents among members. They provide the trust and confidence so crucial to an organization's health. Connections among people infuse the entire organization with energy and ability. When connections are limited or broken, the organization will not have enough energy or talent to sustain itself. It will eventually wither and die.

In fact, in many cases it *is* who you know that helps you "get ahead." When you bring people into the organization, you also bring in the connections they have with the community. When an organizational need arises, it is sometimes a pleasant surprise to find that one of your members knows just the person you need to reach, sort of like finding that 10 dollar bill hidden in your coat pocket.

Relationships between the organization and the broader community are crucial as well. The organization needs to build its network of contacts throughout the community. These contacts help you to get plugged into a larger array of community assets than can exist within your membership alone. Though the organization can make use of its members' relationships with others in the community, it is wise to make connections on its own. In so doing you help create a place for your organization and its work within the community's consciousness. In fact, the only way members become truly empowered is when the work they do through the organization becomes part of community life rather than being done apart from it.

Just bringing people together can produce almost magical results. New ideas are born, new opportunities are seen, and a new belief in possibilities takes hold.

Organized action is all about connecting people to each other and to the issue and to the community. Respect the importance of relationships and act purposefully to form and maintain them. Though the process will vary across cultures, recognize that some time, usually informal, does need to be given over to building relationships. Taking action may help to forge relationships, but in many cases action cannot occur until a relationship has been built. How much of a relationship and how that is developed will vary according to the nature of the situation and the expectations of the people involved, but it cannot be ignored.

Things will be more important to you, the initiator, than to anyone else

Those who initiate change efforts do so somewhat independent of the invitation of others. They have a dream, a special insight, or a particular motive that more or less by itself is sufficient to cause them to act. Those who come along later in the process are either directly invited or decide to join a work in progress. If this difference is not recognized, frustration and misunderstanding, especially over degrees of commitment, can inhibit the change effort.

If you are an initiator, the need for action, maybe even the direction, is clear to you. This sustains you during times of confusion and helps you overcome setbacks. Further, the change effort itself is likely to play a fairly prominent role in your life, even to the point of other matters competing with it for attention rather than the other way around. This will not be true for everyone. You may find it hard to understand why others do not seem as motivated, as quick to understand, or as willing to sacrifice as you are. Explanations range from the type of personality it takes to be an initiator to the degree of perceived self-interest at stake and beyond. The fact is that there is often a difference. It would be a mistake to unconsciously expect other people to attach the same importance to things that you do.

It is helpful to appreciate this phenomenon, but you can go too far in expecting too little from your partners. Others can develop a high degree of commitment to and identification with the effort; some may even meet or surpass your own. Others' sense of determination may be different, but you can act to increase it. Your effectiveness will, to a large extent, relate to your ability to provide opportunities for people to participate at their current level of interest, while at the same time encouraging as many as possible to further develop their stake in the matter. Learn to work with this range of commitment, and acknowledge the contributions people do make rather than where they may fall short of your expectations.

Countering Obstacles to Successful Action

Things never quite work out the way we expect them to. The next set of rules should keep you from being too surprised. These rules may even help you prevent some disappointments, or at least deal with potential frustrations more effectively.

The Rule of 33—things will be 33% different from your best guess

If 12 people told you they would make it to your organizing meeting, expect 8 to show up. If you schedule a project for three months to completion, it will take four. If you believe an activity will cost about $1,000, you better budget an extra $300 or so. Do expect things to be about a third different from what you anticipated, even when you have given yourself some leeway. Also, figure that this difference is not usually for the better.

The estimations we make or the promises we are given are made in the current world, free from the distractions or new developments that lie ahead. We tend to be a bit optimistic in our plans, generally paying a little more attention to the things we want to hear (or what people want to be able to tell us) or the things we have some control over.

If you and your partners are able to recognize this rule as something fairly natural, you will avoid becoming discouraged when actual events don't meet your expectations. So, if fewer people pitch in than promised and things take a little longer or cost more, don't be too surprised. The Rule of 33 is in force. By the way, don't use this axiom to justify reducing your efforts or you may make things even worse.

Expect the ripple effects of change

When contemplating an action you are well advised to first consider its possible repercussions. By asking some questions, you might head off some unpleasant, unintended consequences. Some useful questions are:

- What is likely to happen if we take this particular action?
- Whom might we unintentionally harm?
- Whom might we unintentionally provoke?

Even when you have put some good thought into your planning, you cannot control all the forces acting on a given situation, and even your best analysis is part guesswork. So, come to expect that side effects will be produced by your actions and the changes you implement. This may present you with a new set of problems or with new possibilities for further gain.

Expect that you will need to make adjustments along the way, and don't be surprised to find that when you are all done . . . you really aren't.

Unearned benefits accompany almost every successful change effort

You've had the experience, I'm sure. The group project you had to do in school. The big family dinner with all the relatives gathering to toast Aunt Emma and exchange family news and gossip. And let's not forget the PTA fund-raiser. A number of you are supposed to be working together, but a few are doing more watching than working. Although the project is something everybody will benefit from, only a few of your number really ever lift a finger to help out. Everybody gets something, even the people who don't do anything at all. Unearned benefits. Irritating, isn't it?

The danger to your group is that members may let squabbling over who is not doing what distract them from the business of doing what needs to be done. The goal of keeping people from getting benefits they don't "deserve" may become more important than the goal you started out to achieve in the first place. The group ends up divided and pointing fingers at each other. Hardly a productive way to spend your time, but a temptation some may find too difficult to resist. There may be many reasons why people don't join in the work. Don't assume that you can know them all. Be prepared to learn from a situation in which too few are active. A lack of involvement may indicate that your own actions or inactions are creating barriers to full and meaningful participation. You must be willing to change your style of operation if you expect others to change theirs.

You will be much more effective if you pay attention to what you want to accomplish and to the people who are committed. Put your energy into creating real opportunities for involvement. If the project is truly meaningful and if you are taking genuine steps to distribute work and responsibility, you will find that you have enough support. The help you are able to get is more important than the help you don't get.

Like the Rule of 33, unearned benefits are pretty much a fact of life. When you succeed in making a change, those who worked hard and those who did not receive the same dividends. Some will be happy to let others do all the work, and some won't even know that work is being done. Accept that this will happen and move on.

A religious experience may not last much past the prayer meeting—distractions of the "sinful" world usually prove too tempting

You are all assembled to discuss the situation. Some of you, in fact, are even ready to determine actions that need to be taken. Spirit and enthusiasm run high. People, including you, start making promises about the things they will do to move events forward, down the path of righteousness. You leave excited about all the things that are going to be done. You walk out the door and smack into . . . Kids' Soccer Practice. OK, it may not be anything that serious, it may be your regular job, the faulty bathroom plumbing, or the stack of bills growing like weeds in the "I'll get to it" pile. Whatever it is, it's part of the real world—your real world.

When making commitments regarding your community change project, you may be filled with a sort of holy zeal. You are meeting with other people who have come together to put their faith into action. You all share a common belief about things, and your energy, and perhaps even your guilt, is reinforced by the comments and conversation around you. It is almost as if the real world does not exist or will put itself on hold while you go about the business of promoting change. It doesn't, of course.

You may have membership in many groups. Each of these groups may treat you as if your involvement with them is the only thing you have going on in your life right now. But you have a job that may well have expectations of you apart from your work on the change effort. You may have children who require your time and attention and whose various activities or memberships require your time and attention as well. You may participate in a faith community. You may belong to other community groups. You have friends. You also have to navigate through the routine distractions of day-to-day life. All of this may begin to wear on the sense of purpose that felt so strong when you were last meeting about the change you are working on.

If this description seems to fit you and other members of your organization, deal purposefully with the challenges it poses. You may need to meet more frequently for a shorter amount of time. You may need to keep in touch with one another between meetings to maintain enthusiasm and the freshness of your commitments. Only projects that have a short duration can sustain intensity throughout the life of the effort and push other routine matters off to the side. You may need to recognize that everything will not get done at once and that individuals or even the whole group may have periods of high activity followed by periods of lesser activity. Whatever approach you take, recognize that maintaining your energy and action in the context of other real-world obligations is crucial. To ignore this situation will prove frustrating as promises go unfulfilled and expectations are not met. You may sense that you are not making the progress you hoped for, and relationships among members can become strained. You may find yourselves wondering if you are losing the faith.

Be wary of Sunday social activists and the sneeze experience

Perhaps you have heard about "Sunday Christians." If you adhere to a Christian faith, you have probably heard discussions about such persons. Even if you have not encountered the term, it is likely you have encountered the person: Gets all dressed up Sunday morning, sits in the front pew by choice, nods head knowingly as the sermon progresses, and can even quote scripture. Goes to work on Monday, gossips about coworkers, is a little shy about the truth in business dealings, and generally leaves Sunday far behind.

You may have a variation of the species in your organization. You will know them by their prominence and lack of any real work. They may be seen as activists, but they do little more than talk a good game or show up at meetings all over town. That is, they don't do much beyond going to the services. They would love to do some work for the organization, but, you understand, they are really very busy. (Of course, they have yet another meeting to get to!) So, don't rely on them to do much even though they have the appearance or reputation of activists.

Despite this limitation, they may have some value in that their reputations may provide your organization with a degree of credibility. Be aware, however, that these individuals often have a sort of temporary or occasional affiliation with groups. When their attendance and interest appear to be flagging, you may find yourself worrying how you can keep them involved. This is where the danger lies. You may begin to question yourself and your own legitimacy. You may invest more energy trying to keep a particular person's interest than you put into moving your agenda forward. Don't spend a lot of time fretting about their participation. You will probably have other credible people involved anyway. Go about your business, build your own credibility, and take whatever assistance the Sunday social activist is willing to provide.

The "sneeze experience" is a related concept in that it involves a loss of some participation. After a major event or significant experience in the life of your organization, you may discover the apparent disappearance of a few members. Don't be surprised or overly concerned, but do prepare for this likelihood.

A major event in the change process or an exciting activity is pretty much like a sneeze for some people. It is somewhat dramatic, and once experienced the need or desire to participate has been expelled from their system. The activity can fuel their sense of affiliation with the issue for months or even years to come, even if the activity itself marked the end of their direct participation in the effort.

There are probably scores of explanations for why this occurs, but perhaps just knowing that it does is enough. Avoid being disappointed at some loss, and plan to use the event or experience to draw in new people. Just as a significant or exciting event can complete some members' involvement, it can spur a higher degree of involvement in others.

Each community has its ankle weights, naysayers who need to drag down the unafraid

At the initiation of a change project most participants are a bit hesitant. Some few probably will be pretty enthusiastic, but most are in some state of coming on board.

Working to change a condition requires people first to change their own behavior. That is, they will have to make phone calls they wouldn't ordinarily make, attend meetings they would not otherwise attend, and in general take part in some activities that represent a change in what they routinely do. This requires some investment on their part, some time, some reflection, some problem solving, maybe even some preoccupation.

The payoff must be sufficiently important and sufficiently likely for them to make the investment. At the beginning of the change effort and during the *inevitable* periods of floundering that will occur, that payoff may be highly questionable. Still, if they are sufficiently challenged, intrigued, or encouraged, most will express some interest in helping out.

Then there are those who could take part, but do not. Or they join in for a while, but soon quit. Some of these become the ankle weights. They will frustrate you. Whether this is your first change effort or your hundredth, they will irritate you and impede progress. They may well attend meetings and voice their opinion of the futility or foolishness of the undertaking. A caustic comment or two will be thrown in to general conversations, no doubt to add an important spice to your life.

Although their number may be small, they can drag down a project that is just beginning or that is moving uncertainly. Many participants are likely to have questions about success, and comments from these critics may erode their confidence and commitment. If the members of your group are mostly drawn from a fairly small population, such as members of one church group or one segment of a small town, the rumblings of the doubters may have more effect.

In my experience most ankle weights are just not up to the challenge—but would like to be. They are a bit envious of those who do have the necessary optimism to participate. The call and response to action may threaten their rationalizations about how things are, how things could be, and their role in all this. They seem to be acting out of a kind of self-protection. You probably aren't going to be able to convince them of anything they seem to be doubting, so don't try.

You are not going to gain much either by trying to demean them. That game will produce no winners, although it certainly will distract you from the real work you have to do as well as detract from group morale. It is better to accept the fact that ankle weights are part of the deal. Try to accept them without accepting their negativity.

A few other tips. Don't be defensive; this will only encourage them and get you mad at yourself. Don't accept abusive comments, and don't return any. These occur infrequently, but they do occur. (A "That's not how we discuss things here, Gary" or "Can you say that without making a personal attack?" is usually enough. If it is not, discuss your group's approach with a couple of other members.) Don't spend a lot of time focusing attention on the negative person. Although sensitivity is important, this is not group therapy.

Do address the likelihood of ankle weights at the outset of your effort. If participants anticipate some of this reaction, they are less bothered by it. Instead of trying to justify all your actions, ask critics how they see themselves helping out, perhaps by helping to solve the problems they identify. Be prepared to acknowledge a comment and move on. Do keep your focus on the goals of the group.

We all tend to criticize those things that threaten our interests or our perceptions of ourselves. This tendency will be as true for you as you deal with ankle weights as it is true for how they deal with your work. Treat doubters and supporters within your group with respect. Those who are afraid of the challenges of change may well fear rejection. You can offer invitation by requesting their assistance while not engaging their negativity.

The most powerful obstacles to change are fear, apathy, and ignorance

More than anything else, these three villains—fear, apathy, and ignorance—conspire to keep a group powerless. No group can act with these shackles in place. Heard any of these messages spoken, acted out, or murmured silently in your own head?

> *Fear:* I might fail. I'll look foolish. No one will like me. Someone's going to get mad. I'll lose my job. There's not enough of us. I am alone. It's too overwhelming.
>
> *Apathy:* You can't fight City Hall. Nothing makes a difference. I don't want to get involved. Don't bother me with that, I have enough of my own problems. Let's go get a beer.
>
> *Ignorance:* I don't know how to do this. I don't understand what is really going on. Problem? What problem?

These messages are toxins that mix with each other to debilitate the group. The resulting lack of action seems to confirm the truth of the sentiments. Thankfully, there are antidotes. The antidote to fear is confidence; to apathy, relevant involvement; and to ignorance, learning. All of these are produced through experience, observation, and encouragement. You may need to provoke, irritate, or even cajole some members to help them recognize opportunities for success.

As a change agent you will confront these constraints to some degree in every change episode in which you take part. Accept the fact that these beliefs are present and that they are fairly natural, especially with groups who have had little successful experience acting on their own behalf.

To overcome these obstacles, first act on those things your group does understand and can succeed in. For some groups this may mean that you tackle very small matters indeed. Recognize your group's successes and growing knowledge as you move to successively more challenging tasks.

Each new set of challenges to the organization can call forth these demons from their hiding places. The new is the unknown, the place where these rascals live. As your organization builds a history of confidence and value, these obstacles will shrink fairly quickly from the scene.

So, to the extent that any simple formula can work magic, take the following steps. Bring people together. Begin doing something right away. Tackle issues the group can succeed with, that relate to their interests, and that the group understands. And, all the while, recognize success, encourage learning, and discover potency.

Using Power Powerfully

This set of rules deals with matters of power, addressing the relationship between the issue and the power needed to act on it. I invite you to take a closer look at the concept of power and how it can be used.

You need a base of power equal to, if not greater than, the issue you face

One common frustration for groups endeavoring to promote change is trying to deal with an issue that is beyond their current capacity to effectively manage. That is, the issue is bigger than they are. It is kind of like jumping into the car and trying to drive across the country on half a tank of gas. It just won't work.

The scenario is not surprising. Someone identifies an issue or problem and wants to do something about it. He or she begins trying to make changes. Usually the initiator of action or the issue itself draws other people into the effort. But before too long the drive comes to a stall, and little progress has been made. Sometimes the issue is so daunting that those concerned more or less mill about for weeks or months in meetings, discuss the problem, but take no real action. Looking at the immensity of the matter, they don't know where to start. So, in practice, they never do. The people involved lose heart, and the effort dwindles away, often leaving those desiring change feeling more certain than ever that "you can't get anything done."

Very often this occurs when the issue is defined broadly, such as dealing with child abuse or bringing the town to life or treating employees better. But it can occur even when the issue is more narrowly drawn if those leading the change effort do not recognize the link between power and success.

Whether actually attempting to face an issue or just thinking about the possibility of doing something, those interested in promoting change need to look at the power they now have and the power they think they can muster. Some power is normally present in all situations, but it is generally insufficient to make the kinds of changes people want. Change agents have four choices: (a) give up, (b) build the base of power, (c) break the issue down into more manageable pieces, or (d) combine *b* and *c*.

If you want to proceed past choice *a*, begin by looking at the power you already have and what you can do with it. That is, what do you have going for you that you can actually use to get past whatever forms of resistance you face? Power can include numbers of supporters (willing to voice or act on their support), information, policies or laws that support your objectives, ability to focus and keep attention on the issue, connections with other individuals or groups outside your immediate situation who are willing to use their influence on your behalf, and even the correctness or moral force of your position. Essentially, power involves your control over resources that can overcome barriers presented by the situation and that are valued by those from whom you want to get a response.

Consider the forms of power you have access to or can acquire, and begin drawing it in. Decide how you can get the power you need. Get it, and begin acting, directly taking on only as much as your power will permit. Don't try to take on something you just don't have the power to do.

If you do not have all the power you need—which is usually the case—identify an aspect of the larger issue you can have an impact on and act on this. Broad issues and concerns can be divided into various parts; select one of these parts as your starting point. Pick something sufficiently irritating or interesting that it combines both motivation and power.

You now have put your issue and your power into much better balance. As you continue to move forward, use the issue and your work on it to build your base of power. For example, one group attempting to abolish the death penalty in their state began by eliminating physician involvement in the death penalty. They used this both to draw in physician support for their efforts and to educate other members of the community. They used their success on this piece to work toward eliminating the death penalty for minors and mentally retarded individuals, which in turn brought new awareness and new supporters. They continue to take a piece of the issue at a time, purposefully building power in the process.

Sometimes your opponent may be something much more specific than "conditions." It may be a government agency, a corporation, or another powerful organization, and it may be bigger than you are. Just as you may not be able to take on an entire issue, you may not be able to take on an entire opponent. But you may be able to partialize the opponent by directing your action toward one part of the opponent. This may be a particular division or branch office, a small group of individuals, or even one person. It may be a particular arena of the opponent's action. You select a certain aspect because focused attention on this part of the opposing organization will cause the opponent to respond to you. It may be a part that is willing to be helpful or a part that is vulnerable to confrontation. In either case, maintain your focus; otherwise your power can be dissipated or you may be drawn into a conflict you don't have the power to handle.

"Power with" is at least as important as "power over"

Discussions of power cause many people to retreat. "Power? I don't want to have anything to do with that." Well, actually, you can't avoid it, although you can avoid talking about it. Everything you do involves some use of power. This may be a fairly simple form of power, like taking a walk, or something a little more complex, like you and your friend deciding where you are going to go for that walk. You relate to the use of power, your own and others, every hour of every day of your life.

Perhaps some fear of power is related to how we usually talk about power or how we seem to notice it. Power is often presented in terms of coercion or dominance—that is, people being forced by other people to do something, often against their will. This is one form of power, but only one form. Power can be used to build up as well as to break down. Power can be used to lend a hand in assistance or to raise a hand in anger.

If the only way we think of power is in terms of domination, it may be difficult for us to look at and use our own power. Then, if we don't want to dominate, we don't act powerfully. We become fearful of acknowledging our own direct use of power. We may become more willing to use power in a covert way and to hide it even from our own view.

However, if you can come to understand power in terms of alliance and liberation, you may be more willing to legitimize its use. You can powerfully collaborate with others and you can powerfully break free of rigid thinking that restricts the perceptions of options. You can look for opportunities in the situation to use power in this manner. In some situations this will be more readily apparent or possible than in others.

Dominating power tends to be limiting, preventing people from doing something they want to do. Liberating power tends to be generative, creating new possibilities for people to accomplish their purposes. Each may have its place.

Nothing is more central to promoting change than the ability to generate and use power. It is as simple and as difficult as that. If you want to achieve what is important to you, the use of power will be necessary. This will require that you accept and legitimize its use. Recognizing that you can use power to create with people rather than fight against them may help you look for opportunities to do so.

An effective change agent will help others discover and use their own power

Old notions of power stressed consolidation: "If everyone is acting powerfully, we'll never get anywhere." Contrary to that outmoded belief, in fact, the more people you have acting powerfully and in concert in your organization, the more effective it will be. Acting together is the key.

An organization that can rely on many people will be more effective in the long run than one that can rely on only a few. The organization must outlive the current round of leadership and the current issue if it is to become self-sustaining. Although this may be self-evident when thinking about organizations, it is not evident in practice.

By virtue of previous experience and training or skills needed in the current situation, some individuals are more likely to come to the fore. Unfortunately, they may purposefully or unintentionally block others from asserting themselves. You can recognize this fairly natural tendency and facilitate the growth in influence and ability beyond the group of current leaders.

Commonly, those who bear much of the initial responsibility may not know much about some of the later challenges the organization will face. However, because they are in positions of responsibility, they end up learning. People in this group tend to support each other, particularly when coming upon uncharted ground. Given opportunity, challenge, responsibility, and support, most people can become pretty competent at handling matters.

A change effort demands that a range of things be figured out, decided upon, and done. Members should have many opportunities to recognize and increase their talents as well as their ability to influence other people both inside and outside the organization. An effective change agent will recognize and use these opportunities to promote member competence while responding appropriately to the immediate situation. That is, the change agent will deal with the tasks at hand in a way that builds confidence for handling tasks in the future.

Some people come to the situation with a greater degree of self-confidence than do others. You cannot assume that members who do not assert themselves are uninterested or less qualified. Newer members, especially, may feel less capable than and even somewhat intimidated by more veteran members. Take these factors into account when providing opportunities for increasing capability or influence. Matching people and opportunities will become easier and more routine as you develop your own skills in empowering others.

Helping members to feel a part of the group, especially an important part of the group, is an important step. A feeling of power comes from being a member of a powerful group. Making use of opportunities for members to act as a group, giving an experience of united power, will increase the individual's sense of strength. When people believe in their own power, they value and make more available their contributions to the organization.

Just as members need to build recognition of their competence, the organization itself needs to recognize its competence in handling issues and possessing influence. As your group makes headway on current issues, take note of the power that acting together has given you. When organizations believe in their own power, they value and make more available their contributions to the community.

Fixing blame for the past is less important than taking charge of shaping the future

The point of this business of change is to move forward, not to stay stuck. Fixing blame for the past not only keeps you mired in the situation but conveys a sense of powerlessness as well. It is as if you cannot or need not move forward because of the decisions and actions of others. When you decide to promote change, you are deciding that things can be different and that the decisions and actions of the members of your organization will help make them so.

Blame is different from analysis. Blame seeks to relieve responsibility from oneself and place it on another. Analysis seeks to understand so that one's actions can be more fruitful. In any effective change effort the participants will endeavor to gain a better understanding of the situation. They will look at the antecedents of the current situation as well as those current forces that may have an impact on maintaining or changing conditions. This is done for the purposes of action. Blame is used to justify your condition. Analysis is used to change it.

Practice Wisdom and the Change Process

The final set of rules in this chapter describe a variety of principles that govern the process of change. Each provides an insight on a particular aspect of the change process.

Change requires a sufficiently receptive environment

The arena in which the change is to occur, along with all those people involved in agreeing to the change, either tacitly or explicitly, constitute the environment for change. This arena might be a social service agency, a neighborhood, a professional organization, or even an entire state. For change to occur, this environment must be sufficiently receptive. This is a fundamental premise of community change. If the environment is hostile to the change, the change simply will not occur. Or, if initiated, the change will not be maintained unless coercion is used. Although you may take some actions in a rigidly hostile environment, these actions will not produce a meaningful difference. Thus, actions directed toward softening the environment must be taken either prior to or simultaneous with actions to implement the change itself.

In many change circumstances those promoting the change need to gain approval from those in formal decision-making positions, such as lawmakers or administrators. These individuals must be convinced of the merits of moving in a different direction (or the costs of not doing so). In making their decisions, they will rely on signals from the environment that the change will be accepted or that opposition will be at a level tolerable to the decision maker.

Environments can be characterized as hostile, neutral, receptive, supporting, or promoting. For change to occur, the environment need only be at the receptive stage. Within a typical change environment, a few people will be organized to promote the change, a few people will be opposed to the change, and a lot of people will be somewhere in the middle, either unaware or not much concerned. This vast middle ground includes the real keepers of the status quo. If those in the middle are willing to allow for the change, either through silence or some degree of demonstrated support, the change will succeed if the forces organized to promote the change are greater than those opposed to it. If, however, the middle ground signals opposition to the change, then a high degree of authority or organized power will be necessary for the change to take place. And, even then, the change may be undermined.

It is generally more productive to work to make the environment more receptive than to try to overcome resistance. Education may be an important component in your strategy. Although education itself is normally insufficient to produce change, it may be a necessary precondition that will help move an environment from hostile to receptive. Your educational efforts should be targeted to those with enough authority to permit the change.

Like the soil in a garden, the environment in which your change is to occur must be adequately prepared to allow for it to take root.

You can stop big, but you usually have to start small

Stopping something is easier than bringing something to life. A moderate amount of energy focused on a specific point can be enough to bring things to a halt. You realize this when you drive over a nail. However, bringing something new into being requires a much more sustained effort over a longer period of time. Creating an image on canvas, building a house, even cooking a meal requires attention to a number of steps in a certain order to ensure success. Much less effort is required to frustrate any of these.

So much goes into bringing a project to fruition that a fairly small group of organized activists can thwart an enterprise. Lots of pieces need to fit together and stay in place. As a result, those who want to stop something have many different entry points, many different ways to create delay and difficulty.

Much community organizing involves preventing some change to the community: a roadway here, a housing development there, a waste dump in your backyard. These are all fairly big things. Many big things can be stymied. Just because something seems big, with powerful interests behind it, doesn't mean you can't stop it. Often you can. First, you must make a clear decision to stop whatever it is that you oppose, and you must have organization. In most cases your organization must be able to draw support beyond the circle of the most highly committed activists. Another important piece of the puzzle is information. The more advance warning you have, the better, although you can still put the brakes on something that is well under way.

Let's take a look at some of the reasons things are easier to stop. These reasons can suggest tactics for you to use.

Anything new, especially something big, must answer questions about its benefit to the community. Generally, people do not embrace change. If they are uncertain about something, they normally reject it. Few projects are without some harmful side effects. Emphasizing these can create a climate of confusion and mistrust that will undermine the support the project may need.

The complexity of a major activity is another element working in favor of those who oppose it. It is common that a range of both formal and informal approval must be obtained for things to move forward. Pressure groups have access to these approval providers—for example, elected officials, the news media, or the general public. Further, the malfunction of any component part of the project can bring things to a standstill. Think of how this can happen to your car or your computer. Imagine how this can happen to a complicated undertaking.

When trying to stop something, you have a clearly defined target or issue that can be easily explained to a number of people. This provides a distinct focus for your activities. An identified threat can bring cohesion to diverse sets of interests.

Issues of right and wrong are easier to see. It is likely that there are real, concrete (sometimes literally) examples you can point to. This makes it much easier to galvanize support for opposition, including opposition from a large number of people who only have to be marginally involved in the effort.

Emotions run higher in this sort of situation, particularly strong emotions such as anger or fear of loss. These can move people to action and sustain action.

News media attention is easy to garner. Local news loves controversy. It can shrink a Goliath and build up a David. Public controversy is uncomfortable for those on the defensive.

When you are opposed to something, inaction is a sign of progress. Delays work in your favor, and once something is stopped it is more difficult to restart.

Be aware that some things may appear to be stopped while they are really on hold. If there is enough benefit to people with enough power, they may try again after a period of relative quiet. They may try to wait you out. Don't become paranoid, but do remain observant.

The challenges in implementing something are more difficult but, of course, not impossible. After all, things get done all the time. These challenges can suggest some tactics for you to use.

When you are starting something, you are going from the known to the unknown. This future condition is harder to see than the present circumstances. Thus, the uncertainty works against strong commitment.

It is common for there to be different perceptions of the intended outcome among members of the group working to bring an idea into reality. Even when goals seem clearly defined, these differences can lead to inefficiency and conflict.

Fear of failure is present when trying to make something happen. It just might not work. That "might not" may be enough to dampen the efforts of some of the people you need.

Along with fear of failure is the fear of rejection. Some people will fear others do not approve of what is being proposed or may even think it foolish. Thus, they may not want to appear to be too diligent in their efforts.

The range of emotions in favor of action is important, but often these are not as strong as those evoked by opposition. Hope and excitement are necessary but harder to sustain, especially in the face of adversity. Delays work against you, and enthusiasm can wane.

Change may threaten entrenched interests. These will not always clearly expose themselves, but they can present obstacles, some of which are difficult to see. As you are trying to bring about your change, you may run into the same type of forces you, yourself, might use to stop something.

It is much easier to work on something big by starting out on something small. This allows you to gain some confidence in meeting challenges, and it gives you practice in managing the activities needed for change. The exception to this is if the idea really captures the imagination of enough people willing to commit to it to make it come true. When there is commonly shared excitement and enthusiasm, a community can do wondrous things.

You have four choices when facing a problem situation

When you find yourself troubled by policies or conditions that rankle, realize that you control your reactions. The way you choose to respond will have very real consequences, but the choice is yours.

The first option you can select is to *define the situation as acceptable and decide to accept it.* This is a matter of reframing your perspective on the matter. In truth, not all situations that you initially think are difficult or improper prove to be so. Some aggravating situations can be seen as minor irritations that you decide to live with and not worry about. You would probably drive yourself nuts if you turned every annoyance into a struggle. So some things you can just decide to accept.

Your second choice is to *define the situation as unacceptable and decide to leave it.* You can do this in a very real way by ending a relationship, quitting your job, or moving out of your neighborhood. You can also do this less obviously by remaining formally present while withdrawing any investment in the relationship. For all practical purposes you become invisible. Opting to leave a situation usually occurs when you are no longer interested in improving the situation or when you do not believe you have the power to do so

A third and very common response is to *define the situation as unacceptable and then try to accept it.* This provides a contradiction between belief and action, and it keeps you in a continuing state of disharmony. Complaining is a sign of this reaction. People who act like martyrs are trapped in this contradiction. They stay stuck in their discomfort. This is probably the most unhealthy choice a person can make.

The final alternative is to *define the situation as unacceptable and act to change it.* This is the kind of choice that leads to community change. It can also lead to frustration and burnout if you keep trying to promote change without first building the power to do so. Even if you don't initially succeed, there is some benefit gained simply by knowing you had the integrity to make an effort. Your decision to act conveys a belief in the value and ability of those people who are affected by current conditions. You come to see yourself as a person who matters.

At some point you may need to decide whether you are going to hang onto your problems or work toward a solution.

Three basic attitudes govern a challenging situation: defeat, survival, or success

"High fly ball to centerfield," the announcer intones in a voice almost bored with the inevitable. Watch what the batter does—jogs. Doesn't hustle at all; just jogs. Maybe doesn't even go all the way to first base. Why try? Everybody knows what's going to happen.

Defeat. Many communities are just trotting to first base. They already know that nothing good is going to happen, so why try? Even successes are treated as aberrations. At best they are pleasant surprises or matters of luck that won't last. This is a difficult environment for a change agent.

Some communities are a little bit better off. They are just getting by. Surviving. This reminds me of an acquaintance who, when asked "How are you doing today?" would reply, "Surviving, just surviving." I got the picture of someone spending her life treading water. Communities engaged in an ongoing effort just to keep things from falling apart are in the survival mode. There is some enjoyment in these communities, but such times are temporary breaks from the routine. They are not the routine. Problems are the routine. Although these communities may not be making much observable progress, there is something encouraging about their willingness simply to be engaged.

Some communities meet challenges with an expectation that things are going to turn out pretty well. These communities operate out of an expectation of success. They don't ignore issues, and they don't wait for them to become too big. They act assertively fairly early in the game because they believe they can. Further, these communities are not always stuck with facing problems. Often, they are working to improve, to make things better. Successful communities put forth more effort than less successful communities. This is to be expected. Efforts are perceived as useful. They have been rewarded by results. In these communities setbacks are seen as temporary irritants and are brushed off as something that doesn't fit the community's perception of itself.

So, what orientation do you have? How do you see things? Do you operate out of a perspective that expects defeat, survival, or success? Do your efforts even matter, or is everything that happens outside of your control? Your answers to these questions are important because they affect the way in which you engage your community.

The mere fact that you are reading this book suggests that you believe you have some influence on what happens to you and your community. This is significant because it allows you to see yourself as a contributor.

How much you believe you can contribute and the nature of your actions will be influenced by the attitude you carry into a situation. If the community has a defeatist outlook, and if you don't believe anything is going to be accomplished either, cash in your chips (if you still have any) and call it quits. You are probably wasting each other's time.

The way you approach a situation will have an effect on others, but don't assume that just because you believe in success everyone else will too. It is useful to gauge the prevailing attitude in a community. If the prevailing perspective is defeat, understand that the people in the community may act without much hope. Now, it does no good to get angry over that and directly or indirectly chastise members. That would probably confirm what they already believe to be true. Instead, accept the reality of current beliefs and build toward success in small steps.

A success attitude comes from hope, and hope comes from the belief that something good can be accomplished. Start with a simple goal that people are interested in and that they believe they can achieve. Even when the goal seems rather modest, it is likely that support and encouragement will be necessary. Once some success has been achieved, it is crucial to acknowledge that success and quickly build on it by taking on a little bit bigger challenge. At some point people will start believing that success is a realistic outcome.

Successful communities believe more in their abilities than in their problems. Successful change agents do too.

Change takes time—something we know but assume doesn't apply to our change effort

The principle that change takes time is best appreciated from a distance. In the midst of the struggle, this notion is blurred by a belief that all our doing will be matched by an equal measure of constructive response. Believe it or not, the laws of nature, human nature especially, are not suspended at our request. There are a number of reasons change takes time, beyond the easy belief that those who should respond more quickly are evil or stupid. I'll mention a few. See what you can add to this list on your own. It may help you appraise your situation more accurately.

- All our doing may be less than we want to believe. We are talking and thinking and getting ready to do what we need to do. It sure seems like we are doing an awful lot, but we may not have taken all that many actions.
- What is important to us is less important to other people. They may have other things to which they are giving their attention and energy. Until our actions increase the importance of the issue, we will just be getting whatever is left over.

- We may be convinced of the change, but others may need some time to mull it over. It probably took us some time to get to where we are. It's likely that it will take other people some time as well.
- Some degree of resistance must usually be gotten through. The change may result in somebody having to do more work, do something different, or lose something important. That is, the change may well cost somebody (or several somebodies) something they don't want to give up.
- Everyone will be inefficient to some degree. Not everything will fall into place. Some things will just get dropped, some lost altogether. Some repair, some starting over, and some getting back on track will probably need to occur.

Having a clearer picture of why things take time means we can do some things to speed the process up and some things to prepare for a longer haul than we originally thought.

At the very least, you need to keep from getting discouraged at the slower pace. After you have heard "change takes time" about the third or fourth time, you may want to put a sock in the mouth of whoever is reminding you of this bit of wisdom. Or you may want to go home—so might your supporters. At this point you may want to do a couple of things to keep yourselves motivated. Using your frustration to determine and undertake new actions is one helpful tactic. Another is to focus on specific pieces of the overall change and increase your ability to recognize and call attention to any perceptible gains that are taking place. Still another is to stand back and look at all those small gains together to see that you actually have come some distance from where you first began. In effect you are discovering that significant change is often the accumulation of smaller changes.

A particularly important response is to continue to purposefully develop new leadership, new resources (especially people), and new skills. The slow going will use some things up. Prepare yourselves by having a ready supply of what you need in store.

The fact that something makes sense has very little bearing on what happens

I walked into the meeting, facts in hand. My pitch carefully thought out, well organized, logical. Everything made sense. Couldn't miss.

It did—miss, that is. How could that have happened?

Over the years I have learned a lot about community change, but I seem to relearn this lesson more frequently than I would like to admit. I am getting better though. I am quicker to see when I am expecting agreement based on the fact that things make sense to me. In fact, such a feeling now rings a rather loud bell clanging "CAUTION!"

It is not uncommon to hear people complain when agreement isn't reached: "How can they do (or not do) this? It just doesn't make sense." Yes, it does, although how it "makes sense" may not be understood by looking just at the surface. Usually other matters are at stake.

The notion that something makes sense implies a shared belief in what is important. This assumption can get you into a lot of trouble. You may think everyone agrees on what makes sense because you want to, not because any real agreement exists. Though what is stated among parties may create an impression of common views, sometimes the meanings attached to statements differ, and sometimes the statements are devoid of real meaning altogether. Sometimes people say certain things in public because they simply cannot afford to say what they really think. Yet it is what they really think or, perhaps more accurately, feel that will direct what they do. There are even times when people haven't yet figured out what they believe to be important. For want of anything better to do, they give the appearance of cooperation. When the time comes for decision or action, the issue is forced and what earlier seemed to "make sense" becomes irrelevant to what's really going on now.

What really makes sense may come down to who does or does not like whom? Who feels a loss or gain of turf? Who has an old axe to grind or a new wedge to drive?

To make matters worse, I have been known to feel pretty much finished with an idea once it makes sense to me. I may have struggled to reach some particular understanding, but then I expect others not only to arrive at the same conclusion but to do so with much less struggle. I understand it now, and so should they. I'm not sure whether this is ignorance or arrogance. Probably a little of both.

Having worked so hard to get to wherever it is I've gotten, I'm not so eager to hear that I'm in the wrong place after all. Rather than taking another look at my own position, it may be easier to label people who can't see how my views make sense as confused or even foolish.

Given all this, it is amazing that very often things make enough sense to enough people with diverse interests that they finally agree to implement an idea. Now, when I don't get the agreement I expected, I'm a little less surprised than I used to be. I've learned to step back and take another look at why people may be balking at implementing an idea that seems very logical to me. This helps me see what the real target of my attention ought to be.

The secret to life is good timing

You've probably heard that before. It's true in comedy, in cooking, and certainly in community action. *When* to act may be as important as *what* you do.

Two particular aspects of timing are important to change agents. The first relates to the disposition of those whom you intend to influence. The second concerns what you have at your disposal that you can use. Recognizing how the second relates to the first may be the secret to success. These things can change over time.

The people you are trying to influence probably have a number of things at any given moment that they would consider important. They are not going to do anything about you unless you have their attention. You may or may not be able to keep their attention for very long, but you probably won't be able to keep their attention forever. After a while they may just get used to you. Your tactics have to take advantage of your target's current inclination to respond. If you act too early, the target may not have established a sufficient connection between your aims and theirs. If you act too late, the tension (creative or otherwise) necessary for action may have passed. Frankly, you need to act when the target is ready to, not when you are. So you get ready first.

(By the way, the "target" is simply the person or group of persons to whom you are directing your actions and are intending to influence. Targets may be either friendly or unfriendly.)

Your tactics may be geared to steadily increasing the target's inclination to respond, with you prepared to take your major action when interest is at its peak. Or you may decide to catch your target off guard so that it reacts more reflexively than thoughtfully, with you poised to capitalize on this reaction.

The target's inclination to respond is related to how it perceives what you have to offer. This is where the second concern, what you have at your disposal, comes into play. Generate resources that can influence the target. These may be public support, active membership, information, ability to make good on threats, or any other thing that might be meaningful to the target. Whatever it is, you have to have it if you want the target to respond to you. So, attract attention only when you can respond in a meaningful way.

Once you have accumulated some valued assets, you are in position to act when the timing is right. Although you may be able to foster favorable conditions through your own actions, be prepared to capitalize on opportunities presented to you by the environment. For example, you can take advantage of an emerging climate of public concern or make use of some unexpected incident to provoke the target's reaction. You may not want to let situations like these pass.

There may be times when members of your group want to act before they have anything to offer but emotion. You may have few numbers, little organization, no clear position, or no meaningful connections to the community. In short, you are not ready. Though you want your group to become impassioned and to express emotions, it must do so productively. Frustration can occur if the group has no way to vent emotions. But frustration can also occur if venting emotions directly toward the target produces no meaningful response. This may present you with a tough dilemma. You may have to hold off direct action and focus your energy on discovering or generating some resource that is of sufficient interest to the target. Or you may be able to direct the emotion to some very specific matter where results can be easily achieved. The point is that you cannot take significant action before you have something significant to offer.

The more you can match what you have available to the inclination of the target to respond at a particular time, the more likely you are to be successful. If you really don't have what you need in a situation, it is usually better to let the opportunity pass or to modify your goals to match your resources.

A moderate challenge is better than those that are too hard or too easy

Sixth grade, Mrs. Wogan's class. She loves poetry. You try, but you cannot quite comprehend the benefits of standing up in front of the class reciting lines of cadence and rhyme—from memory no less. Mrs. Wogan does, however, and she's the teacher. Still, she is accommodating, so you get to pick your own poem to memorize. Gee, thanks. So what do you do? Probably you pick something between "Rime of the Ancient Mariner" and "Roses Are Red," a little closer to the "Roses Are Red" side. It's got to have enough lines, but not too many to remember. It can't be too childish, but you have to pretty much understand what it means. That is, it has to be a moderate challenge.

Things that are too difficult hold the prospect of failure. We avoid them. Things that are too easy are ignored. They don't attract our interest or our energy. This is true whether selecting a sixth-grade poem or determining a plan of action for your organization.

The goal your organization decides to pursue and its related activities must be within the group's perceived ability to accomplish. Yet it must represent a sufficient break from the ordinary that the group feels tested in some way. Scale things up or down, organizing tasks with the appropriate blend of trial and simplicity. That is, remember your own Mrs. Wogan when helping to set your organization's immediate aim.

Pay due regard to the three Holy M's: the message, the medium, and the market

Communication itself is a process that intends a response; that is, information is sent with the expectation that those who receive it will do something with it. Examine the messages you sent today. Did you say good morning to a member of your family? Maybe you discussed the morning's news with your colleague as the two of you took part in your daily coffee ritual. You might have sent a memo to your supervisor about the need for upgraded software. In each instance your message contained within it some subtle or direct expectation of a response.

In promoting change we are busily engaged in the business of communicating, usually with a pretty clear intent that our messages will somehow influence another's understanding and, eventually, behavior. However, these messages often don't have the impact we would like. In fact it sometimes seems that nobody is listening. Why is that?

Well, sometimes it is precisely because people aren't listening. When people aren't listening, it may be because we haven't put much thought into what they will hear. We have started at the wrong end. We have started with what we want to say, and we may be much more interested in our saying than in their hearing. To get more of the responses you're looking for, start with the market, not the message. Paying purposeful attention to the three Holy M's will help you get the message out.

The market.   These are the people you are attempting to influence. You may think of them as your audience. It is likely that on any one issue you will need to reach a number of different groups or segments of the overall public. Do you know who they are and what they would listen to?

By clearly identifying the groups that may support or oppose your desired change, you will know whom to target with what message. Some of these groups will require more direct attention than others. You should also have a good idea of others who may react to what you do and say. When you identify each group's interest in the matter, you are well on your way to relating effectively to them.

The medium.   Think back over the last week or so. What information did you receive that affected what you thought or did about something? At the same time you probably missed some information and ignored other information altogether. How did the way this information was delivered affect whether or not you responded to it?

In my home state, a liberal politician recently offered some ideas for dealing with teenage pregnancy that sounded like a page out of a conservative handbook. The leading liberal paper editorialized on the merits of his ideas. I could not help thinking that if a conservative lawmaker had said the same things the paper would have dismissed the suggestions out of hand. What seems to matter most in some situations is not *what* is said but *who* is saying it. To put it more broadly, the link between the market and the message is usually of vital importance.

The medium is the way in which the message is delivered to the market. This may be anything from a person-to-person conversation to a news story to a highly technical position paper. Three aspects of the medium are important to bear in mind. First, the credibility of the source for the particular market: Does the market believe this particular source to be reliable? Second, the appropriateness of the means of communicating the message: Is this the sort of vehicle that the particular market would expect to deliver this type of message? Third, the existing connection between the method you are using and the people you are trying to reach: Does the market regularly tune in to this particular medium?

If the linkage between the market and the message is solid and reliable, your information will get through, otherwise you might as well be howling at the moon.

The message.   Your understanding of the groups you are trying to reach will help you craft the messages you send. Just as the market is segmented, so too will be your message; that is, you will emphasize different points to different groups. For example, one group may respond well to the cost-saving element of the change you are proposing. Another group may be more interested in hearing about its effect on children. I hope it is obvious that you will not mislead, nor will you obscure the fact that you intend to accomplish a change. The core of your message will stay the same, but various aspects of it will be emphasized for different groups.

When you send a message, you are purposefully trying to produce an intended response. You are not just saying what you want to say. You are saying what people need to hear to respond. This requires both discipline and careful thought. Ask yourself these questions:

- What groups are we trying to influence?
- How do we want them to respond?
- What do they need to hear to respond in the way we would like?
- What is the best way for each group to receive the message intended for them?

On a good day the world operates 65% on form and 35% on substance

I always think back to the times when adults spoke to a group of us teenagers about something or another that was for our own good. It may even have been. But they didn't succeed in getting their message across. How they talked to us got in the way of what they were trying to say. Invariably they used slang that was just a bit too old, and they never could get it quite right. In the end we seemed to remember more about how out of touch they were with us than the message they were trying communicate.

If you get your form wrong, nobody will pay much attention to your substance.

Another memory. I was saying good-bye to my daughter, who was about four and a half at the time, as I was leaving to work out of town. It just so happened that I was meeting some elected officials upon my arrival, so I was suitably attired in coat and tie. My hair was cut. My moustache was trimmed. Even my new shoes were shined to make a military officer proud. My daughter laughed at me. She asked me why I was wearing a costume. (At this point it would be accurate for the reader to conclude that my normal garb was, well, a bit more casual.) I had to explain that I was a lobbyist and this is how lobbyists dressed. Otherwise, people wouldn't take seriously the things I was saying. She listened patiently, and when I was done she asked, "Are other people going to laugh at you too?" I don't think she really got the point.

If you get your form wrong, nobody will pay much attention to your substance.

The way we present ourselves, our issues, or our information can help or interfere with how these are received. Dazzle and style are often more powerful than content and can ease or frustrate acceptance of your ideas.

There are times when putting on a good show is necessary. Indeed, sometimes it may even be more important than what the show is about. The presentation creates the impact. The show itself can give or take away the legitimacy of the subject. Frankly, the overall impression often is remembered long past particular facts.

Inattention to your form conveys a disregard for your audience. It implies that what may be important to them does not matter to you, while what matters to you should be important to them. A little arrogant, isn't it?

People do not connect with ideas that are presented in a language or in a form that is inaccessible to them. Barriers may be created by presentations that are too complex, too condescending, or too boring. People are also put off by laxity or carelessness. When your manner is sloppy, the credibility of your ideas will suffer. If your approach to people is poorly done, your ideas have to walk through a minefield of resistance. Do give some attention to your form. The substance of your effort will thank you. Maybe this shouldn't matter—but it does.

So, if you are going to have a press conference, do it right. If you are going to testify before a legislative committee, be prepared. If you are going to organize a demonstration, put on a good show. Ultimately this is about communication.

You don't need to suggest a solution to identify a problem

You may have heard something like this: "If you don't have a solution, you can't complain." Yes I can. What an absurd philosophy. Can you imagine visiting the doctor when you aren't feeling well, describing your discomforts, and hearing the doctor respond, "Well, what's your solution?"

The no solution, no complaint sentiment is a sure way to preserve the status quo. It can also lead to picking apart any solution that may be proposed. This can turn into a very big game. Those "in charge" may pose a less desirable alternative as a "solution." Or, you may be asked for a solution when you clearly do not have the power to implement it. Then there is the ploy of requiring you to suggest a new direction when there is obviously no genuine support for exploring its merits. This can all be very frustrating, silencing direct criticism and pushing it not away but underground.

It is perfectly legitimate to note that something isn't going well even if you aren't sure how to fix things. The problem and the solution are two different things. You may know one very well without having an equal insight into the other.

Having said that, I do believe you have some responsibility to participate in developing the solution to the problems you identify. Demonstrating your willingness to do so gives legitimacy to your complaint and increases the chance that the solution will be to your liking. You do not have to have a solution to bring a problem to light, but you do, I believe, have to be willing to work out the solution to the problem. If asked "Do you have a solution?" you can say, "No, but I'd be willing to work with you on one."

Your actions may well create discomfort

The companion of change is uncertainty. That alone can be uncomfortable. Change requires that we step out of routine patterns of seeing, thinking, feeling, and doing. Though these patterns may themselves be troublesome, we are at least used to them. Like it or not, we have learned them, and we probably are pretty good at them. Change asks us to exchange something we're pretty good at for something we may know little about. This can be unnerving. It can even keep us from mustering enough energy to make our good intentions come true.

There are other discomforts beyond uncertainty. For some, change may result in a real loss of power, status, prerogatives, money, relationships, or other resources that people have come to value. Struggling against such losses will produce resistance, which is often expressed in conflict.

As a change agent, you may not want people to feel bad. You may want change to occur without anyone really getting angry or hurt feelings. You may be reticent to upset those who are holding tightly to or trying to gain that which is not rightfully theirs. You may be so unwilling to provoke discomfort that you are willing to perpetuate it through inaction, in effect asking those who are now unhappy or dissatisfied to remain so.

You must come to grips with this and accept the fact that change brings some degree of discomfort to some people. Maybe even a lot of discomfort to a lot of people. Remember, though, that discomfort with the way things are, felt by enough people, led to seeking a change in the first place.

A change that is put in place may not stay in place

You may have worked hard to finally get something accomplished, to introduce a new change in an area of your life that is important to you.

Congratulations! But your work's not done. The power of tradition and old habits may very well undo what you have done. It may happen fairly soon too.

Remember that commitment you made to exercise? How long did that last? How about the time you decided for sure that you would balance your checkbook after every check you wrote? Should we even bring up the diet? Which one?

Communities have habits just like people do. They also have interests that may have accepted a new change only as a temporary condition until they can figure out how they can change the change. You developed good support to see that the change was made; now you need support to see that the change remains in place or is improved on. You can't dig a hole and plant a rosebush and leave it alone, and you can't put your change in place and expect it to root and survive without any attention.

There are some things you can do to make it more likely that your change will be firmly established. Perhaps the most important work you can do to confirm your success occurs during the organizing to put the change through in the first place. If you have developed a broad investment in the effort, you will be in pretty good shape. The more and varied your supporters are, the more interest there will be in maintaining what you have accomplished. Further, opponents will be less willing or able to undermine your gains.

Once the change is made, vigilant monitoring is required to see that agreements are kept and that the innovation receives adequate attention. You will need to do this until the new patterns have become pretty routine. You will also need to use or take advantage of the change you have introduced. If things are put in place but are not used, they do not become part of the life of the community, and there is little reason to keep them around.

By paying careful attention to what you have brought to life, you will see it survive and mature. The hours or years of effort to produce something new will have been worth it.

The work of community change is really the work of small groups

"Community change" sounds like a tall order. How can you make a change affecting so many people? Even a community of only 100 people can be a lot of people. How can you get anything done? Well, there may be lots of people, but you only work with a little bit of the community at any one time.

First of all, only a segment of the community generally is concerned enough, one way or the other, to become active in the change process. Of this number only a small percentage will be highly active, and even those members will rarely all work together at the same time in the same place. You may, and you should, have many people involved in working for the change, but they will principally be involved as members of a particular group. The entire organization will come together only for special events or planned actions. On these occasions the main obligation of members is simply to show up and take part in the activity. The real work is done in small groups.

In most change situations, not only will a relatively small percentage of the population be interested in the issue but an even smaller percentage will need to be actively organized. Depending on the size of your community, this number could be less than 5% of the population. This organized group will be able to reach out to other members of the community as needed, mobilizing more of the community for a specific action. It is likely that this group will divide itself into various teams or committees, each of which will focus on a particular aspect of the change effort. So when we talk about organizing a community to promote change, understand that only a small portion of that community will be tightly organized and an even smaller number will routinely get together at any one time.

This raises the importance of understanding how small groups work and developing skills so that these groups can work effectively. Two books on this subject that I have found particularly helpful are *Joining Together* and *Group Process: Theory and Experience* (both appear among the readings listed at the end of the book). The points I will touch on are drawn from these books as well as from my own work.

The small group is the primary mechanism for moving the change process forward. It provides some structure to both the key concerns and the work of individuals, and it links these to processes within the community that are targets of the change or that could be supportive of the change. Further, in an organized change effort, the small group both directs and encourages the work that needs to be done.

In most change efforts the work is done by members of a team or by the team acting together. Individual work includes basic activities such as phone calling, letter writing, various forms of data gathering, and similar activities. The work of groups generally falls into one of three categories: specific task performance (addressing envelopes, making signs, or planting trees), meetings with those outside the organization (elected officials, business owners, and other community decision makers), and decision making.

It is this last category, decision making, that may well be considered the heart of the organization. Groups within the organization analyze the information being gathered and come to decisions regarding the overall strategy as well as the next steps that should be taken. This set of decisions relates primarily to the goals of the organization. Another set of decisions relates to internal matters, such as the structure of the organization or internal problems, including conflicts among members.

For a group to accomplish its work and make decisions, it must develop and use resources effectively and efficiently and take care of itself. Groups operate on two levels simultaneously. The first of these levels is the work or task level. This involves all those conversations, decisions, and actions directly related to the work the organization is doing. The focus here is on the goal the organization is trying to reach. The second level is the relationship or maintenance level. This involves all those conversations, decisions, and actions directly related to how people in the organization are working together and getting along. The focus here is on the people in the organization, their relationships, and the degree and manner of their participation.

Effective groups pay attention to both domains of group functioning and balance their attention. Groups that are too task-oriented will eventually fall apart because they haven't taken care of themselves. Groups that are too relationship-oriented won't get much done. Part of this overall balance involves knowing when to concentrate more on task activities and when to address relationship activities. Groups with a limited focus that do not intend to remain together for very long are likely to have a much stronger work or task orientation.

All the while a group is functioning on its task and maintenance levels, it is going through stages of development. These stages are normal for an action group. One simple way of depicting these processes has been described by Tuckman and Jensen (see the readings list for their work on this topic). They identify the periods in the group's life as forming, storming, norming, performing, and adjourning. That is, groups spend some time getting themselves acquainted with one another and their purpose. Then there is a time when members try to assert themselves toward one another and rebel against the authority figures of the group. Next, comes a period when the group's procedures and manner of relating to one another are worked out. This is followed by a concentration on the work of the group. Finally, when the group has accomplished its purpose, it may terminate or start a new project.

Healthy groups are likely to go through these stages, and they revisit earlier stages when issues from a previous stage resurface. Unhealthy groups get stuck in stages without moving forward. A miniversion of this developmental sequence takes place every time a group gets together. All this progress through stages is very natural, but it can get complicated. You may want to explore this subject further. Much has been written about it.

A few other matters of small-group work are worth mentioning here. Groups need to meet the needs of the individuals who belong to them. Some of the most important needs are those involving the need to feel included; the need to have control over what happens; the need to receive and express affection; the need to be recognized as an individual and to be recognized for achievement; the need to work, to create, and to accomplish; the need to play; and the need to express care and concern for the welfare of others. Strong and effective participation comes when members are able to meet these needs.

Actively invite participation: One of the more significant and easy things to do is to invite people to share their ideas and to participate in discussions. Those who are a little shy or uncertain about what is being discussed may need this invitation. Also, you will probably need to invite people to participate in the work of the organization. For various reasons some members will hang back, allowing others to do work they could be doing. Effective groups will have full participation.

Distribute leadership: Different people can provide different forms of leadership required by the group. Some leadership will be directed to the work domain of the group and some will be directed to the relationship domain. No one will be able to provide all the leadership necessary. Leadership is an action or set of actions; it is not a person. Any action that influences members of the group to move forward on either the task or maintenance level is a leadership action. Encourage all members of the group to engage in these actions.

Use time wisely: The group affirms its existence when it spends time together. Time should be well used so members recognize that their time together produces progress in accomplishing their goals or strengthening their relationships.

Communicate effectively: Necessary information needs to be given and received. This is much easier said than done. The members need to practice saying things in a way that other members can clearly understand and respond to productively. Information must be communicated in a way that can be used. Members should make sure that the messages they send are also clearly received.

Manage conflicts constructively: Conflicts are natural. They need to be acknowledged and openly addressed by recognizing the legitimate interests of those involved and the goals of the group. Not every little conflict needs to be exaggerated into a major crisis. Effective groups learn that conflicts are routine and can be handled routinely. They can be used to strengthen the group or to weaken it. Conflicts are normal; they are neither good nor bad. The way the group handles them can be effective (good) or ineffective (bad).

Promote group ownership and pursuit of goals: Goals should be decided on by the whole group, not just by one or two members. Once goals are established, they should be used to provide direction for the group. All actions should logically be related to the group's stated goal, not some other unstated goal. If action is routinely directed to other matters, the group may need to revise its goals.

Remain flexible: Encourage members not to get stuck in one position. Members need to be willing to see how changes to their ideas, positions, and plans can help the group accomplish its goals.

Accept the fact that confusion will occur: Lack of certainty can create fear among members. Members need to believe in their individual and group ability to figure things out. Confusion will occur. The group simply needs to acknowledge that state and then decide to act to be unconfused.

Certainly there are many other tips for promoting the effectiveness of small groups. However, if you recognize the normal needs of a group and its members and you attend purposefully to them, you will find that your group works well and that the work of the organization will advance.

It may be easier than you think

Our fear that things won't work out is often the most significant obstacle to our success. It weakens our resolve, reduces our effort, and pares down the number and type of actions we take.

You may have to get used to the idea that you can make things happen. People who decide to act and do so purposefully and persistently produce improvements. I have seen this many times. Those of you who are just getting started may not have witnessed many examples of success, so you may not be so convinced of this proposition.

Of course, the smaller or more narrow the change you seek, the more likely you will be able to see some progress. (There's a hint for you.) If you are attempting to change policies that are well entrenched or patterns of behavior that are strongly ingrained or widespread, you will need to make a significant, sustained effort. However, many community change possibilities exist wherein resistance is insignificant or unorganized.

Our assessment of the difficulty of producing change may be related to our experiences with attempts that didn't seem to go anywhere. Many of us, for example, have complained about a situation only to see problems persist. We might conclude from this that "nothing can be done." A more accurate conclusion is that complaining doesn't work. Complaining is not the same as purposeful, persistent, organized action (even action involving just a few people). Complaining is usually limited to voicing discomfort, and often it is directed to those (for example, a colleague or friend) who are not in a position to do anything about the matter. Organized action is geared to producing resolution, or comfort, if you will, and it is directed to or with those who can do something. Complaining is passive and temporary. Willful action is assertive and sustained.

Another issue to consider is the tendency to overcomplicate things. Sometimes we tie ourselves up with activities that pass for action but that aren't clearly linked to moving forward—endless meetings, unnecessarily elaborate procedures for decision making, or maybe even the ever-popular paralysis by analysis. We may take so much time getting ready for action that when the time comes for action we have lost our enthusiasm and our troops.

Community change is not the product of some set of mysterious rituals. It is not nearly as baffling as you might think. Certainly, some aspects of change, such as economic development or legislative lobbying, require particular knowledge, and some skill areas, such as fund-raising or media relations, come with their own bag of tricks. However, you need not be stymied because you haven't yet solved these mysteries yourself. If you need such specialized expertise, you can usually find it. With further training and experience, you too can discover how primary development brings more new dollars into an economy. You can learn what would be the best day for your story to break in the newspapers.

The fundamental work of community change does not commonly call for mastery of esoteric skills. You need to engage more in diligent work rather than difficult work.

CHAPTER 4

Things to Know About Yourself

You might ask, "Where do I start?" The first step to initiating change in your community is to change what you, yourself, are doing. Becoming a change agent or increasing your skill as a change agent is fundamentally about making changes in what you see and what you do.

The rules offered in this chapter have made me much more effective. More often than not they reflect changes I had to make in myself, how I approached the challenges that working for change presented to me. Some of these challenges involved temptations to yield to bitterness, frustration, or simple laziness. Observing my ineffectiveness or the ineffectiveness of other change agents led me to formulate many of these rules.

Don't be afraid so much of discovering your ineffectiveness as of hiding from it. Get into the habit of reflecting on the quality of your work. Discover what you do well and what you do to get in your own way. Notice how you respond emotionally, cognitively, and behaviorally and how your responses help or hinder what you are trying to do.

You will have doubts. Doubts about your effectiveness. Doubts about your group's chances for success. Doubts about the wisdom of your involvement given the personal risks you must take. All change agents have these doubts, and many others. Develop support from other activists and others actively involved in the effort. Accept encouragement. Remind yourself of the importance of the issue. Remember courage.

No set of rules can keep you from making mistakes. You will learn a lot through your mistakes, and you will probably do the right thing more often than not. There will be times when you act quite capably, even brilliantly. There will be occasions when you catch yourself (or not) before you do something really stupid. Grab on to these learning experiences. Running smack into a brick wall may teach you the importance of alternative approaches to getting to the other side, but using the doorway can teach you this as well.

Too great a fear of doing it wrong will lead to inaction. Give yourself permission to act. In so doing you will make mistakes. You will also do things effectively. Give yourself an orientation toward discovery. A strong emphasis on learning is liberating and leads to effectiveness. Add a few more of your own personal rules to this list.

The single most important thing you can bring to any change effort is yourself—your values, your personality, your intelligence, your insights, and your actions. Do not underestimate your contributions to the change effort.

This chapter provides a set of rules that will help you think about how your own attitudes and actions affect the prospects for change. Understanding options for how you can act and react to a variety of situations and challenges can help you act more purposefully. First, let's consider some underlying themes that shape your effectiveness as a change agent.

Your effectiveness as a change agent is directly related to your ability to promote agreement.   Agreements produce transactions—the giving and receiving of things tangible, like money, and things intangible, like permission. Change is the product of transactions. Purposeful change is the product of purposeful transactions. Your ability to handle disagreements effectively and avoid actions that hinder agreements will lead to productive transactions. The rules identify a number of factors that will help you reach agreements among members of your group as well as between your group and others.

Your effectiveness as a change agent depends on some constructive aspect of relationships.   You will need to manage relationships in a way that strengthens your organization and furthers its interests. It is particularly important that you act in a way that promotes the involvement and the investment of others. The rules encourage you to take a look at the things you can do to help this process—or to *not* get in your own way.

Your effectiveness as a change agent requires you to accept the realities you face.   Face reality, not a contrived picture of it. Avoid forcing your own expectations onto a situation, especially without challenging them. Otherwise you will become frustrated, unable or unwilling to move if reality does not conform to your expectations. Taking an honest look at a situation includes not making up problems that don't really exist and not making those that do exist bigger than they really are. The rules will help you deal directly with the world around you in a way that is realistic and based on optimism.

Your effectiveness as a change agent requires that you act with both creativity and discipline.   A change agent who is willing to do the unexpected will avoid becoming predictable. Creativity will enliven your efforts and expose an expanding series of possibilities. Humor and irreverence can loosen the invisible bonds that sometimes hold us back from invention. Change often resists the dullness of the ordinary. Imaginative approaches can render useless the often used tired responses while keeping things fresh and fun for your participants.

A change agent whose ego is in check will avoid self-serving mistakes. Acting intentionally will help produce the outcomes you want. The rules describe some traps you can fall into and suggest how self-awareness can be a fundamental asset.

Your effectiveness as a change agent is closely linked with your ability to make conscious decisions about the nature and degree of your commitment to the effort. You cannot be halfhearted and fully effective. Also, you can rarely put the rest of your life on hold while you pursue the change you are working on. The rules offer guidance for managing your involvement with the real demands of a change effort along with your other responsibilities.

As you consider these themes, understand that the ways you relate to the people in the change effort, to the change effort itself, to the entire challenge to promote change, and to your own increased self-awareness will go along way toward increasing your effectiveness. Challenge your own limited view of things, and make use of the myriad opportunities for learning. Avoid setting arbitrary limits on yourself, and actively challenge the real limitations you face. Recognize, believe in, and build on your strengths. Your personal effectiveness in promoting community change—your awareness and your actions—is largely within your control. It is as much a matter of decision as it is skill. Once you decide, you will build the skills you need. Keep deciding.

How You Relate to People

This set of rules invites you to take a close look at the actions you take toward other people. Notice the common pitfalls—along with some good ways to avoid them.

Prevent yourself from contracting the disease of being right

"What a bunch of idiots," you're thinking as you shake your head, not really trying to hide a smirk. "Apparently they don't know anything," you conclude. Now it's time to let them know how stupid they really are. You begin your response in the tolerant tone reserved for fools. Great formula for working out an agreement—or is it?

If you are afflicted with the disease of being right, you listen to catch people in error, and you want to show them they've been caught. You listen to point out flaws. Agreement means other people agreeing with you. Those in the advanced stages of the disease cannot handle divergent points of view, kind of like lactose intolerance, though it's disagreement they cannot stomach, not milk. Different opinions are not just different, they are faulty, and it is somehow the sacred duty of those afflicted with the disease to let holders of these different opinions know just how faulty they are. If you are right and have to be right, then any idea that varies from yours must by definition be . . . wrong.

No doubt you have been on the receiving end of this behavior. (It's much easier to notice from that perspective.) Maybe it was your boss, your drill sergeant, your teacher, or even your dad who could be so adept at putting you in your place. How effectively do you relate to people who are intent on showing you that you are wrong? How able are you to listen thoughtfully to what they have to say? How willing are you to agree with them and let them know it?

The disease of being right is not to be confused with having firm convictions. A strong faith in your beliefs does not necessarily mean that other beliefs are without merit. In fact, the more secure you are with your ability to examine your own beliefs, the more likely you are to acknowledge others. In the arena of community change, you will be able to draw from other points of view to build an understanding that can be more broadly accepted.

Certainly, strong opinions, dispute, and disagreement are a frequent part of attempts at community change. There may well be multiple interests at stake. Yet it is the effective management of disagreement that often holds the key to implementing change. Success ultimately relies on a series of agreements among parties. Agreements are made through the discovery of common ground, not the undermining of it.

A change agent with the disease of being right seeks to discredit. A change agent with firm convictions seeks to accomplish.

Listen as aggressively as you speak

Have you ever watched two people arguing and think that they are talking over, under, around, but certainly not with each other? You sometimes think they aren't even speaking the same language, much less talking about the same subject. Does anyone ever watch you do this?

A helpful treatment for the disease of being right is to hold yourself to the same standards that you want to hold other people to. When you are working hard to get your point across, do you expect (demand?) the other party to really listen to you? How many times have you said "Just listen" to someone else? How many times have you said those same words to yourself? Do you work just as hard at getting *their* point as you do when making your own? What might be the effect of doing or not doing this?

When you listen to others, how do you do it? Do you listen for things they say that might support your argument, maybe even using their own words against them? Or, do you listen to understand what is really important to them? Do you pin them down on their mistakes, or do you pin down what is true for them? When someone says "Yes, but" to you, what do you hear? When you say it to them, what do they hear?

If you do make a sincere effort to clearly understand what someone else is trying to say without filtering it through your own point of view, how would they know this? It doesn't matter if they *should* know it; it only matters that they *do* know it. Hone your listening skills

Obviously, the more you are in disagreement, the more difficult good listening is. But this may be precisely the time when it is most important. If you demonstrate that the way out of this disagreement is for one party to finally beat down the other, kind of knock them down into verbal submission, what do you think the outcome of the discussion will be? If you demonstrate that each party should expect both to hear and to be heard, what outcome would you predict?

Wouldn't it be nice if in the middle of a disagreement the other party would describe just what you are really trying to say in a way that let you know they genuinely understood? Here's a test. Can you state their position in a way that is satisfactory to them as well as you can state your own position in a way that is satisfactory to you?

Declare your needs in a way that people can act on them

He sits there, arms across his chest, scowling at the television screen. It's Martha Stewart demonstrating imaginative ways to fold napkins for a semiformal garden party. You suspect he's not really paying attention.

Just as you begin thinking about a row of cloth ducks floating on the red-wood table outside, you realize that you don't have garden parties, semi-formal or otherwise, and that your only napkins come in packages of 250 from Safeway. You also realize something is wrong with that man over there. "You don't look too happy, Bill. What's goin' on? Are you upset because we always use paper instead of cloth?" Your attempt at humor falls as flat as that no-yeast bread Martha convinced you to bake last fall, so you try again. "Really, Bill, what's bothering you?" He looks at you, shakes his head, turns back to Martha, and says, "Nuthin'." This is going to be a long afternoon.

If you, your group, or Bill are going to get a response from others to help you meet your needs, you have to let other people know what those needs are. Now, you and Bill may decide to play this game of making them guess, or you might even move the conversation to an argument about the fact that they should know. However, this may not be entirely productive in getting an efficient response.

Declaring your needs is a starting point, bringing out into the open what you require but don't have. However, the way you do this is also important. Not only do you want people to know what your needs are but you want them to act to help you meet them. Ideally, you would act so that it is easy for them to help.

Here are three common mistakes groups often make when asking for what they need. The first is to act as if they have little or no right to make a request. They more or less apologize for what they need and imply that no help would really, well, after all, be, I guess, okay. Not a very compelling approach. The second error is to attack the source of help before giving the source the opportunity to respond. This method presupposes rejection and punishes the potential offender before the transgression even occurs. Of course, this is likely to set up the rejection that is feared in the first place. The third frequent mistake involves asking the wrong question, something like this: "Why can't you help us?" You may very well get an answer to the question, but you may not get anything else. "How can you help us?" might lead to a more fruitful discussion.

For people to respond to you they have to know what you need, and they have to be in a frame of mind to give it to you. Attending to both these matters is likely to be much more productive than "nuthin'."

You can't hold people accountable for things they don't know

A tornado is ripping its way eastward through the cornfield, right toward the little farmhouse where you're staying. You hear some noise, so you look out the opposite window of the living room. "It's a little stormy out there," you think, "but maybe the rain will be good for the crops. Glad I'm indoors, safe and dry." You go back to the recliner and Oprah. You're in for a rude awakening . . . or maybe a big sleep.

Things don't exist for you unless you know them. Sure, they may actually exist, and that existence may have consequences for you, but there is nothing you can do about it if you don't know it's out there. Just as this is true for you, it is true for everyone else actually or potentially involved in the change effort.

Ignorance is a powerful ally of the status quo. You will be amazed at the lack of awareness that exists among policy makers whose decisions have an impact on your situation. Though they may be otherwise well informed, you may find that their knowledge does not extend to the matters you are facing. It may be completely foreign territory to them. Even people who live in the midst of problems may not recognize them. They can be living ankle deep in mud and just think they are having a little difficulty walking.

You may want these people to respond, but they can't. They don't know enough. Just because you understand a situation doesn't mean that someone else does. It does little good to expect or demand action from someone who doesn't really know what you are talking about. You very well may need to introduce those from whom you want a response to the situation that requires their response. You may need to both educate and demand, but do get the order right.

Ignorance can serve as a kind of protection. Some people don't go to the doctor because they don't want to find out that they are sick. This doesn't change the fact that they are sick, but for a time it does keep them from having to deal with the emotions and behavioral changes that the knowledge of illness might require. Some people are afraid to take their car into the shop; others are afraid to step on the scale. A lot of us work real hard at not finding out things we don't want to deal with. When people in a position of power do this to avoid dealing with problems in a community, they can and should be held accountable for their willingness to remain ignorant.

It is particularly important to be patient with members of your own organization, including the leadership. Unnecessary internal disputes can be created out of what someone should have known or done. A little informing before attacking can save a lot of disruption.

If you don't know something, you cannot act on it. If someone else doesn't know something, you cannot expect them to act on it either. You may hold people accountable for clinging to ignorance, but you cannot expect them to act on something outside of their awareness.

Don't bad-mouth people

You have just heard some pretty unflattering remarks about someone, unfortunately they are about you. Actually, your friend has just told you what he overheard at a meeting. Seems everybody laughed. Feels great, doesn't it?

Those snide remarks, those comments—cruel but so clever—how often they come back to haunt you. They always seem to get back to the person you're talking about. It's like blowing up a balloon and then just letting it go. Once you let it go, you don't know where it will end up or what it will look like when it gets there. A friend of mine who is a press secretary with years of experience once told me, "If you can't handle reading it in the morning paper, don't say it." Good advice. If there is a comment you don't want traced back to you, don't make it.

The tendency can be hard to resist. You do get angry. There are jerks and buffoons. But what's the point? How do you really benefit from running somebody down? There is a good chance that the world will discover whatever shortcomings you may feel compelled to comment on anyway. It's hard to politely greet someone whom you have trashed behind their back, especially if both of you are aware that has occurred. You come off as a phony, someone not to be relied on.

I suppose we need to dehumanize our enemies to some extent. It may make it easier when we have to plan and take action that places them in discomfort. We may also need to remind ourselves of who the "us" is by diminishing the "them." Locker rooms are full of quotes from opposing teams tacked up on the wall by coaches who use these comments to motivate the players. If you do not want your remarks used in that fashion, maybe you shouldn't offer them in the first place.

We don't always reserve our cutting observations for declared enemies. Sometimes we do it to allies or potential allies. It's just not very productive.

Now, you don't have to be the Keeper of All Things Wonderful and Mannerly when a group you are involved with begins trashing someone who happens not to be there. (This *will* happen.) Though you might try to change the subject, it may be enough just not to participate. Over time you will notice that people come to respect you more, perceiving both strength and safety. It is not one of those showy kinds of qualities, but there is something of substance that is appreciated.

Never, ever bad-mouth a member of your own organization. Doing so weakens you to those outside the organization and plants seeds of doubt within the organization.

Derogatory comments are just unnecessary. These are the racist jokes of the community action game. They serve much the same purpose, to put down one group in favor of another, to show relationships of superiority and inferiority, to make the different bad. Nonpurposeful ridicule is a sign of fear. Bad-mouthing other people cheapens us as much as it does our targets. If it becomes a habit, it can affect the way we think about people and relate to them. You can be a tough opponent or a reliable ally, but don't be seen as cheap.

Effective community change requires some degree of discipline. Keeping a handle on what you say about people is a good place to start.

If you allow people to let you do all the work, they probably will

It's just too hard to explain what needs to be done, why, and how. Anyway, this is pretty important, and you want to make sure it not only gets done but that it gets done right. So, you might as well just do it yourself.

Do you ever hear yourself thinking these things? If you have ever felt some degree of responsibility for a project, my guess is that these thoughts have tempted you more than once or twice. I bet you have even given in to the temptation on occasion. We all have.

Members in an organization, like you and I, don't usually mind when someone offers to take some work off our hands. If you just went ahead and did things without ever mentioning what needed to be done, everyone would let you because they didn't actually have a choice in the matter. After a while, though, most would probably decide that there's nothing for them to do, and they'd stop being involved.

A good change agent will make sure that a growing number of participants take on more and more responsibilities. By increasing participant experience and competence, leaders and other members have a sense of confidence that any number of people can handle a particular job. Further, more members become willing to initiate activities or provide good ideas on how affairs can be handled.

There is no real harm to your assuming disproportionate responsibility every now and then. However, doing it once may lead to two times or three or four, or. . . . It's easy to establish a pretty damaging pattern here. What are the outcomes of such a pattern? "Well, for one thing, I could make sure some things do get done the way I want them to." Good. What else? "Maybe, after a while, others in the organization will become kind of disassociated with the work of the enterprise. Their sense of connection to the effort may dwindle and they may drift away." Right. And? "And they end up getting used to not doing much work and feel burdened or maybe even put out if they have to take on some responsibilities."

What about leadership? "I guess the circle of leaders and key workers will get smaller and the roles more rigidly defined. Maybe even to the point of being a little organization unto ourselves. This would probably limit input into decision making, even reducing the number of ideas we could use, wouldn't it?" Yes, it probably would.

How about for you? "For me?" Yes, you. "Eventually there could be a lot on my shoulders, and I'd look at the other members and feel pretty resentful that they aren't carrying their share. Also, with all there is to do, I may not do a very good job (gasp!). I may end up not liking the work very much or the organization very much, and if I stick around, which would be questionable, I might hear myself complaining a lot. I may not have as much time as I would like with my friends and family, and their understanding of my being busy all the time may fade more than a little bit. I may not be very fun to be around."

Very good. It seems like you've got a handle on this. Now, are you ready to act on those insightful answers? "Pretty soon. Just let me get this mailing out first."

Avoid taking up too much room in a conversation or in the action of the group

In your eagerness to get things done or get things started, it is likely that you will have a lot of ideas, and some sense of direction. You may have more anger or more enthusiasm than some of the others who have come to take part in the change effort. Without intending to do so, it is very easy to dominate a discussion or decide to handle many more of the organization's matters than you should.

Imagine that you are moving into a new house with a number of other people. You bring your microwave, your television, your stereo, your pool table, your collection of condensed books from Reader's Digest, and a few thousand other things. You cram the closets with your designer-label clothes. You stock the shelves with your canned sushi. And you fill the fridge with gallons of yogurt and four months' worth of take-out leftovers. All this stuff may be pretty good, but you may clutter up the place. There may be no room for anybody else's belongings. You can squeeze them out. They probably won't live with you for long.

Listen to your conversations. Who is doing the talking? Look at the work being done. Who is doing it? If other people are not contributing, it's probably because they have learned there is no room.

Create space, and invite other people to bring their goods.

How You Look at the Challenge of Change

The two rules in this set address some fundamental perspectives on change to ground you in reality while they encourage your purpose.

Take the world as it is, not as it should be— then move it to where it should be

This is a notion expressed by Saul Alinsky as he described a "realistic radical." It is an orientation that opens you up to action: "Given this is how things are, what can I do?" It is simple and straightforward and gets you further than "Things aren't right, why do people have to act that way?" (As if an explanation would make things better.) There is more than a hint of being overwhelmed in the second question, a feeling of powerlessness, as well as an implied resentment for action. "If everyone would just be nice, I wouldn't have to do anything. Now look at all the work I have to do!" There are too many resentful change agents on the scene who are stuck in their own frustration because of their unwillingness to accept the current reality as a starting point for action. They want the starting point to be much farther down the road than it is. Well, it's not, and no amount of railing at the fact will change it. Doing what needs to be done in this imperfect world will.

Expectation and hope are two different things. Expectation involves a simple prediction of what will happen. It takes a look at current circumstances and answers the question, "What is likely to occur here?" Hope involves optimism. While recognizing the current reality, hope offers a belief that better things can occur. These different, better things represent a change from current reality. That change is the result of desire and purposeful action, not desire alone.

Being well grounded in how "the world is" can be liberating. It will free you from the sometimes paralyzing frustration that results from expecting (that is, predicting) the unlikely or impossible. We cannot expect things to be different simply because we don't like the way things are now. We cannot expect people to act differently than they normally do.

What *should* happen and what is *likely* to happen are two different things. Getting these confused will drive you crazy.

There is something to be said for treating something the way you want it to be, influencing it positively through your behavior and optimism. This is intentional action purposefully directed toward promoting change. It is designed to produce a particular response, it doesn't just assume one. It is a tactic based on the recognition of a potential difficulty in the situation. It accepts the difficulty as real and responds accordingly.

Dealing with a world that isn't makes your actions irrelevant to the world that is. Though you may keep yourself apart in a sort of moral smugness, treating the world as it should be rather than how it is amounts to living in fantasy. When that fantasy does not live up to your dreams, you get angry at it.

By the way, the world as it is isn't all bad. Seeing the world clearly allows you to regard obstacles and assets alike. There are things that bother you and things that make you smile. Uncluttered by false expectations, you can operate with an attitude of clarity, honesty, intention, and hope. A pretty potent combination.

Accept the fact of certain conditions, not the inevitability of them

I accept the fact of poverty. I accept the fact of racism. I accept the fact of domestic violence, child abuse, and a hundred other afflictions that diminish us all. But I do not accept that these always must be.

Afflictions such as these are not etched into the permanent foundation of our humanity. They were not put there outside of our control, impervious to our action. We made them up. We can unmake them. True, acting on ourselves, transforming how we perceive and behave, may be much more difficult than reshaping something apart from ourselves. And, yes, total and complete nirvana probably won't be experienced for another month or two . . . maybe longer. Nonetheless, conditions can and do change. Change agents recognize this.

Nothing we create is permanent. This is true for the pyramids, and it is true for our social problems. We can imbue them with a false power that is almost godlike, but they are not gods. They are creatures of human design. Though they may be powerful, they still depend on us for their daily sustenance and continued existence. That means we can do something about them.

I have no illusions that the most significant problems we face will be easy to dismantle. But that awareness is not sufficient to dissuade me from participating in the task. The gains I see may not seem terribly significant in the overall scheme of things. Yet they are gains, and they are significant in the lives of the people who are affected.

The big problems may one day fade from existence, but even less permanent and more subject to change are those issues I can see right around me, growing like weeds in my own backyard. I may not get them all this weekend or the next, but ultimately, if I keep at it, there will be more lawn than weeds.

Many things confront and confound us. Some of these began long ago and some will continue beyond my lifetime. But some others can be removed from our present and placed in our history.

I do believe we are capable of being stronger in our strength than we are mean in our weakness. That our ability is more enduring than our inability. I recognize that the problems we face are real, but they are not immutable.

Poverty, racism, violence—this may be "how things are." It is not "how things must be."

How You Relate to the Change Effort

This particular set of rules will help you understand how you might relate to the demands of the change effort itself. Your decisions regarding the nature and extent of your involvement in change, as well as the effect your participation has on you and others, are covered here. Finally, I provide some tips for promoting your own personal effectiveness.

If the issue is important, you will have to act *as if it is*

Not another meeting. Maybe I can just stay for an hour, tell them I have to be somewhere else. Oh, and those phone calls. I hope nobody's in and I can just leave a message on the machine.

Ever had sentiments like these? You have made a commitment to a group, then you try to do as little as possible while still fulfilling that commitment. You don't feel quite right because you believe in the cause, but you would really rather not have to do very much. The sense of dissonance is even worse when the cause is something that is very important to you. So, you go through the motions of commitment, doing what has to be done, though you seem to fight it every inch of the way. You are caught between the decision to be involved and the decision to avoid involvement.

I once worked for the County Highway Department. (I use the term "worked" loosely.) Being young and having been counseled well by my father in the virtues of citizenship and hard work, I tore earth with pick and shovel at an impressive rate—for a week. My fellow crew members, veterans of this brotherhood, were decidedly not impressed. When it became clear that I was slow in picking up their more subtle messages, they sat me down for a little "discussion." Let's just say they impressed upon me the virtues of a more, uh, reasonable pace. It all had something to do with making sure there was enough work to keep everyone employed and no one exhausted.

I soon mastered the art of looking busy without really doing very much. I became good at turning 2 hours of work into a day-long enterprise. I did a very good job at avoiding work. I adapted and became an accepted member of the fraternity.

A curious thing happened. Any work I really had to do became much more burdensome. I felt put upon when I actually had to work more than half a day. I devoted a lot to my performance, spending energy just to keep the charade going. At the end of the day I was more tired than I had been that first week.

Whatever job you face, trying to avoid the work takes work, and it doesn't leave you feeling very satisfied, especially if progress is slowed. If the issue truly is important to you and you know that work has to be done, accept that fact, don't fight it. Trying to keep your involvement at arm's length from your life will lead you to resenting the work and performing it poorly.

There is a difference between not wanting to do the work and not being able to (though in our less honest moments we can miss the distinction). If the matter really requires your attention, do give it what it needs, without thought of how little will be enough. Otherwise it will never seem like "little" and it will never seem like "enough," and you will be annoyed with it. Accepting your role and performing it capably will make the work much easier and more rewarding.

When you are actually limited by other equally worthy obligations, you may need to define your involvement according to the interest, time, and energy you really have. The fact is that something has to give somewhere. When the matter is at a critical point, or if it is very important to you, some other obligation may need to be dropped or put on hold. You can overtax your interest, time, and energy for a short time for some specific situations, but beyond these you will begin to resent the expectations you have created.

Not that many issues will be critically important to you. In your volunteer involvements there will usually be a good deal of opportunity to tailor or renegotiate your level of responsibility. Avoid assuming roles that are likely to grow beyond what you intend to do. However, on those issues that directly affect your interests or that you are keenly concerned about, you will find that deliberate acceptance of your responsibilities is much easier and more effective than fighting them.

To say "yes" to something is to say "no" to something else

This business of community change can be seductive. As your involvement in the community grows, so does your awareness of various possibilities and initiatives for solving community problems or developing community strengths. With a crooked finger and a smile, each beckons you to follow it home . . . maybe just for a little while. If the beguiling nature of these issues weren't enough, their supporters are actively trying to get you involved, often resorting to the shameless use of bald-faced flattery. These temptations can be hard to resist.

Just say no. At least to some. Don't worry, you will be asked again.

If your participation is to mean anything, it will require not only your time but a bit of your heart as well. That is, your involvement should mean something to you as well as to the change effort itself. The time and energy you put into this project cannot be put into something else. Saying "yes" means saying "no." This is a very basic notion, and actually rather simple, yet it is hard for some community activists to grasp.

Imagine that you can juggle three bowling pins pretty well. Four takes some doing. Five is definitely the limit. What happens when you let somebody toss you a sixth? As you gain experience, your juggling skills will grow, but still there will be a limit, not the least of which is that you don't want to spend your whole life juggling. When you do say yes, you have to be ready to say no to something else. Do be aware of that. It will make your yes's really mean something.

Pick the hills you're going to fight on

There are only about four billion truly worthy causes that could benefit from your participation. You will say yes to some of these. Thank-you. Among those you decide to work on, your level of affiliation will vary and you will treat your attachments unequally, reserving your most dedicated involvement to only one or two. Even within these, few matters will require your absolute commitment, but there will be some. These are places of little compromise and total dedication. These are the hills you will fight on, the places you take your stand.

Be selective about the battles you choose to fight. The decision to fight must be followed by the decision to fight unequivocally and effectively. Taking on all challenges or making everything a fight will leave you more exhausted than successful. Further, looking for battles everywhere will turn everything into a battle, whether it deserves to be or not. You could lose perspective, and supporters and opponents alike will be unable to know when to take you and your issues seriously. Eventually they won't take anything you do or say seriously. Not every issue nor every aspect of every issue is worth going to the mat for. Spending all your time rolling around on the floor is not an inspiring sight.

Occasionally you will be called to face up to a challenge with unwavering determination, to take risks, to know courage. These are times when adhering to your principles and your purpose demand your excellence and your unflinching resolve. Not everything is worth fighting for, but some things are. Know the difference. Pick your hills.

Be willing to be surprised

"Yes? How can you say yes? I'm not sure what you mean." Dropping the pencil back to the pad marked with clownish sketches of the man sitting across the table from him, Mort leans back against the chair.

"Just 'yes,' Mort. That's all. We'll do it."

"Not so fast, Larry. I need to think about this."

Four months of wrangling seemed to have left Mort and Larry firmly planted on opposite sides of the table, and the issue. As the representative of Citizens for Environmental Quality, Mort had agreed to one more meeting to give Larry and Adamson Development Corporation one last chance to agree to CEQ's final proposal. Ready to launch attacks in the media, the courts, and before the County Commissioners, Mort was prepared for them to turn him down. But they didn't.

"Now what am I supposed to do?" he wonders. Mort is only ready to know Larry and Adamson as enemies. Comfortable in that arrangement, he is undone by the prospect of agreement. It would not be surprising if Mort allows everything to unravel, even to the point of actively undermining the agreement, so he can get back to more familiar ground.

Some individuals assume no opposition to their suggestions and are thrown off when resistance pops up. This is less common for those who have been active for a while in promoting change, but it is fairly frequent for those making an initial attempt to offer improvements to a situation. More common are change agents who are stuck in their focus on disagreement. This is what they know. They seem unable to move toward agreement. It's like a new country with languages and customs all its own. They don't know how to act when they get there, so they avoid the destination. In both cases these players have defined the reality of their situation in very limited terms and cannot tolerate the emergence of a reality that does not fit this definition.

True, in conflict situations opponents often veil duplicity behind the appearance of agreement. So accept an apparent sudden change of heart with some caution. Yet, for reasons noble or otherwise, opponents do change their minds. They do act differently from what we might expect. The curious thing is that we want them to act differently, but we may not allow that if it occurs.

Even in situations not dominated by conflict, you may find that you do not readily accept anything out of the ordinary. Good ideas and a willingness to help seems to come from only a handful of people. You can place people and events into some pretty confining categories and dismiss any behavior or occurrence that does not fit your preordained perception.

It is easy to confine people to a role, locking them in an invisible box from which you won't allow them to escape. You may not like how others act and react in situations, but you also may not permit them to be any different. After a while they may only know life in the box and be afraid to step outside it. You may be afraid of them doing so as well. What are you going to do if they try?

Count on the fact that events will unfold differently from what you had planned, and that some specific things will happen that you did not expect at all. When you are uncertain, you may find that you are more ready to accept the reality of bad surprises than good ones. Do be well prepared to deal with either.

You have to be pretty flexible to allow for surprises. You have to emotionally as well as intellectually understand that you don't fully control events or people and that your perceptions may be faulty. These are things that some people know but do not believe.

Remaining open to the unexpected allows you to recognize and capitalize on unanticipated opportunities. It also keeps you from becoming too rattled when a problem suddenly surfaces.

We create dragons that we then have to slay

Dragons aren't real. We make them up to bring our dull lives some excitement, or to scare the bejeebees out of someone, generally peasants
and small children. Nonetheless, dragons have spawned a good deal of
literature and millions of colorful parade costumes. We still spend a lot
of time and energy on dragons.

Not as exotic as the original versions, but apparently as menacing,
are those dragons we create while working on a change project. They can
still inspire anger and trepidation. It is somewhat mesmerizing to see
them being born, hatching from their otherwise meager disguises. What
starts out as a missed deadline becomes NOBODY GETS ANYTHING DONE! The
meeting that produced only yet another meeting turns into NOTHING IS
WORKING! And the quote in the paper from the opposition reveals itself as
MY GOD! DID YOU SEE WHAT WE'RE UP AGAINST!?

You can give life to a dragon simply by believing you see one.
Dragon creators can be identified by the tightly fixed look that gives
them a rather narrow view of things. Some even say that this causes
them to magnify the very size of the monster itself. Who knows? Could
be true.

By making the problem bigger than it might otherwise appear, the
dragon creator can successfully bring a lot of work to a halt. You see,
dragons need to be fed. They have quite an appetite. They regularly con-
sume a great deal of worry, some time, and a fair amount of energy.
They are very good at absorbing attention as well. This is good for dis-
tracting you and your colleagues from other more routine work that
waits to be done.

It's hard to slay a dragon all by yourself. Your alarm will usually call
others from the work they were doing so they can worry about, describe,
and discuss the monster. All of you may even make elaborate plans for
bringing the dragon to its knees to end the threat. In fact, if you do see a
dragon, it would be a shame for it to go unnoticed by those around you.
So, getting others riled up about it may be very important to you.

Unfortunately, when bringing the creature to life or when attacking
it, you may knock off a few of your allies. Often this occurs when, apparently in a moment of hallucination, you see them as part of the monster.
You may lop off a few heads with the swinging arc of your cutting words
or chase a few off with your frenzy before you come to your senses. This,
of course, makes the dragon even bigger.

Now that you have created the dragon and everybody has seen it, you
really do need to do something to get rid of it. During the time of its ex-

istence, you may not realize how hard it is to get rid of something you have put together yourself. There are two basic ways for doing this. First, see what you can learn from the situation out of which the dragon emerged, then take concerted action to bring it down to size. Second, stop feeding it.

During periods of stress that accompany every change effort, you may get a little goofy. It's during these times that you and those around you might create dragons. Understand that this isn't out of the ordinary. Go a little easy on each other and the dragons won't get out of hand.

Don't set arbitrary limits on yourself

Have you ever been on a scavenger hunt? You know the sort of thing where you have a list of peculiar items you need to gather, usually something on the order of the left shoe of a banded gecko or maybe just a matchbook from a convenience store. You look at the list, shake your head, and say to yourself, "This is ridiculous, I can never get this stuff." It's an odd task to be doing, but it's not impossible. If you don't give up right away, you will find yourself checking many items off your list. You'll notice that it's easier than you had thought and that you are having fun in the process.

You've got a meeting across town in 20 minutes. If you leave now, you'll just make it. (The town is not that big.) It's important that you be there. You hop in your car, turn the key, and are greeted with one click and then, *dead silence*. You pause, this couldn't be happening, and try again. Same result. Dead silence, dead battery. What's your next step? What would you do in this situation? Would you be one of the too many who would just call and say, "I can't make it. I have a dead battery." What other choices do you have? Sometimes we have to break out of our consternation to consider any options at all. We don't even begin to think about how we can challenge this situation, we just fume at it.

"We can't do that." You have heard those words before, haven't you? Maybe you thought them yourself even if you didn't say them out loud. You know what I mean. You can't picket. You can't disrupt a meeting by singing the theme from *Gilligan's Island*. You can't meet at 6 A.M. You can't bring out the TV and newspapers to call attention to a problem swept under the rug. You can't do any number of things. Bunk. Who says so?

It is not uncommon for people to draw neat little lines around what they are allowed to do, even what they are capable of doing, and then complain that they feel hemmed in. They see no options in the little pen they have created for themselves, but they don't even think about stepping outside it. Many of the limitations we feel are of our own making. We simply make up things we can't do and then get mad at our limited options.

When confronted with a frustrating situation, you might think of the problem rather than thinking of the options. If so, you stay with the problem. You're stuck. Considering options opens up possibilities for things to be different. The more creative your consideration of options, the more possibilities you will have. You cannot decide what course to pursue unless you have a number of courses to consider. Just because you can do something, though, doesn't mean you should. Maybe singing the *Gilligan's Island* theme isn't such a great idea. Yes, you could do it, but maybe it won't produce the outcome you want. So, what else is there? You may choose not to do some things, but do give yourself the chance to decide. Some situations are so entrenched that the routine options don't work. You need to think of options beyond the options, things that are not routine, things you don't normally think of doing. And if you are in a conflict, think about things your opponent wouldn't think you would do either. Give yourself a chance to solve the problem. If you don't ever challenge your assumptions, there is nothing you can do. If you stay with "this is impossible," it will be.

The fact is that you can do many, many things in most situations. The number of possibilities is limited only by your creativity. Further, you are far more capable than you may give yourself credit for. You have probably had a number of "this isn't so hard after all" experiences. Can you imagine how many people are routinely using E-mail today who were intimidated by the prospect just a few months ago? What kinds of things have you learned to do after you got past telling yourself that you couldn't?

Setting arbitrary limits on ourselves is very common. I am frequently surprised by how often I do it myself. The routine is very powerful. We have to get used to challenging it.

"Now, sit right back and you'll hear a tale. . . ." You can't do that? Who said so?

Understand that your purpose is to be effective

Understand that your purpose is to be effective, not cautious (though this may be important), not loud (though this may be necessary), not fired (though this may be fruitful). Your purpose is to be effective. Your purpose is to produce some intended result.

All of your actions or inactions are geared toward making something happen. The way you act or the reactions you produce are designed to make progress toward your goal. Anything you do that is not related to your goal is irrelevant or substitutes another goal for your primary one.

Some people working for change get caught up in a way of being, or confuse an event for an outcome. For example, I have seen social workers refusing to directly confront an abusive system because acting otherwise would seem "unprofessional." I have seen a congressman's office occupied in a rather bizarre fashion mainly because some members of the occupying group didn't have anything better to do at the time. An attitude or strategic orientation is adopted because it takes advantage of opportunities present in the situation. An action is taken not because it is important in and of itself but because it strengthens the group or moves the group closer to accomplishing its goal. An action may be avoided because doing so would be a waste of time or would expose the group to unneeded risk. Taking or avoiding action is intentional.

Pay attention to the keys to personal effectiveness

As a change agent you have certain responsibilities that may exceed those of the general membership. Your decisions and actions will have a significant impact on setting the tone and direction of the effort. When you engage in action, you do so purposefully to help the group get closer to its goal. In your role as a change agent this is what you are all about. Five keys to personal effectiveness can help you achieve your goal:

- Adopt a success attitude
- Be prepared
- Acknowledge people and what they say
- Follow through on your commitments, thoroughly and on time
- Say thank-you

Adopt a success attitude.   Assume victory. You have felt this before. You know you are going to hand that paper in on time even though it's due in 48 hours and you haven't yet written the first word. You're shooting a little pool and are down four balls, but you've just begun to chalk up your cue. Your brother just called because his car won't start; you know you'll get it running.

In some aspect of your life you have had that conviction, that feeling that things are ultimately going to work out. You aren't sure just how you are going to make it happen, you just assume that you will. With such confidence you can brush aside setbacks.

It may take some experience with community change to develop quite the same level of confidence, though you can borrow the feeling from other life experiences to get you started. Adopting a success attitude means that you will trust in your ability to figure things out. When you begin by assuming that you will ultimately succeed, that belief alone is more meaningful than any particular thing that happens along the way.

Be prepared.   Do you ever get the feeling that *most* people prepare for a meeting by reading the minutes of the previous meeting on the way over? Have you ever gone to a public demonstration where the organizers were more or less figuring things out on the spot? How often have you shown up to begin some activity only to hear, "Now what are we supposed to be doing?"

I have stopped being amazed at how regularly people are unprepared to engage in the activity they expect to do. I have seen people sit down to a negotiating session with no discernable strategy beyond "let's get what we want and not get manipulated into giving up too much." I have seen planning sessions lead to yet more planning sessions because "we don't really have the data we need." I have seen people who are well prepared with information and a strategy for using it make a huge impact, far disproportionate to their apparent power, simply because they were so much better prepared than anyone else.

Some time in advance of the activity, think about what it is you want the activity to produce: What needs to happen to produce it? Who needs to do what? Include how you will proceed in the face of something unexpected, what other people not in your group are likely to do, and what you need to bring with you to make it all happen. These are not difficult or mysterious things to deal with. They are pretty straightforward. Some purposeful forethought and preparation will accomplish a great deal more than making things up on the spot.

Acknowledge people and what they say.   It feels good to know you have been heard, doesn't it? Even if you did not get agreement, the fact of being heard leaves you knowing you are part of what is taking place. There's a sense of connection, that you fit somehow. You may have had other experiences as well. Ever feel that what you have to say somehow loses weight and seems to drop to the floor halfway between you and the person you were speaking to? You might as well be a piece of furniture in the room. For all practical purposes you don't count much beyond being a prop in somebody else's play.

Acknowledging what someone else has to say is one of the most elo-quent things you can do. We may not want to stand out from or above others, but we want to matter somehow. When you take someone seri-ously, you remove the need for her or him to struggle, perhaps ineffec-tively, to do that all alone. You may also keep them from giving up on the effort too easily. The respect you show makes it more likely that respect will be returned.

You don't need to agree with someone to acknowledge her or his point. What is important is that the person know he or she has been heard. It can be helpful for you to repeat the message and your under-standing of its importance.

It's nice to hear the sound of your name when you or your ideas are being recognized. (Yes, there are exceptions to this having to do with irate bosses and your mom using your first *and* middle name.) Do learn people's names and use them. It may take a little effort, but make a con-scious decision to do so. (By the way, do people who "just can't remem-ber people's names" think they are much more or much less important than the people whose names they "just can't remember"?)

Follow through on your commitments, thoroughly and on time.   You will hear the refrain "It's in process" more often than you will ever care to recall. Roughly translated this means: "Shoot, I forgot I was supposed to get that done until you just now reminded me. I'll get working on that pretty soon, I think." Don't learn that phrase.

There is a corollary to this rule, which is "don't promise more than you can deliver." You have probably gone to one of those all-you-can-eat establishments. You wade through 14 different types of salad and 9 veg-etable offerings before you get to the good stuff. Fortunately, you did bring two plates for your trip down the serving line. You nudge the sweet and sour chicken to make room for the ham so you can say "yes, just a small piece" (wink) to the carver standing over the prime roast beef. And you still have the "make your own sundae" and apple pie to contend with.

It is just as easy to make some fairly simple sounding commitments during a meeting. When you actually sit down to do the work, you look at what you have piled up on your plate and wonder, "How am I ever go-ing to get through all this?" Keep your commitments meaningful and reasonable given the demands of the project and other things you have going on in your life. You certainly can challenge yourself to make more than a minimum contribution, though you may want to place just one plate on your tray.

When you agree to do something, do the work completely. Make sure you accomplish the full intent of the assignment. Further, finish the job on time. Getting things done when you say you're going to get them done and getting them done well helps move the project forward more steadily. When you do this as a matter of routine, not to show off, you quietly demonstrate an expected level of performance for participants. This example can be catching. It can influence how the organization develops its expectations concerning the authenticity of commitments.

Say thank-you.   You have heard this before. This action is commonly appreciated, but uncommonly practiced. Certainly it is not done in proportion to the number of genuine contributions people make. Yet it is such a simple thing to do. Thank-you's might be assumed, but they are certain when they are mentioned.

Most important, a thank-you acknowledges the other party and any investment another party has made in your relationship and your work. That investment could be something significant, such as dollars or a specific action on your behalf. It could also involve something as simple as someone giving you their time just to listen to what you have to say. A thank-you represents the recognition of value, which communicates a practical awareness of something important to both parties.

This giving and receiving provides some basis for a relationship. Thank-you's affirm that transaction and the fact of a relationship. Because everything happens through relationships, your actions to take notice of relationships, even seemingly minor ones, and to strengthen them, gives your work a firmer foundation.

Saying thank-you may be used to complete an action. It can allow the parties to put something of their relationship into their shared history, which may help them move into the future.

Expressing appreciation is important even when you do not receive what you had hoped for. You may, for example, be turned down for a grant, or someone may make a contact for you that doesn't produce the results you had wanted. In both cases your interests have been considered, even if not met. It is sometimes the act of consideration or the intent to assist that you can acknowledge, rather than the actual outcome. In most cases you will have reason to work with people on more than one occasion. Acknowledging your relationship when you didn't receive an immediate, obvious benefit can be important.

Acknowledgment can be given just as easily for the mention of an idea as for a donation of a sum of money. The thank-you can be simple or elaborate. Whether it be a nod of the head, a personal note, or an appreciation banquet, any contribution to the effort should receive a thank-you.

Expressing appreciation recognizes and encourages positive intent and solidifies relationships. It affects how you look at people. It also affects how people look at you. Saying thank-you can reduce tensions in difficult situations and accelerate good feelings in more agreeable ones. It is one more step to take, but it is an easy one. Saying thank-you will set you apart from those not saying it. Your future work will thank you for it.

If you do these five things, you will be far more effective than most activists. There is quite a difference between being involved and being effective.

 ## General Self-Awareness

The most effective thing you can contribute to the change effort is yourself. The more you know about yourself—how you act and react in certain situations—the more effective a change agent you will be. In fact, nothing is more important to your participation than your self-awareness. These rules provide a final set of things to consider in gaining self-awareness.

We all fall victim to listening for things we want to hear

You are in the middle of some community change episode. Maybe there is some resistance. Maybe things are kind of floundering. Maybe you are not getting much help. What is it that you want to hear? You had better be aware of it, because you may want it bad enough that you will hear it even if it hasn't really been said.

"That's a good point, we'll look into it." Nope. Sorry. That's not an agreement. "Yes, I hear you." Huh-uh. There has been no commitment to change anything. "Yes, I'll help." That probably can be understood as something less than staying up day and night, licking stamps, writing press releases, scrubbing floors, and taking out a second mortgage on the house until this thing is done.

You may be offered a little flattery to keep you from being forceful. You may hear things designed to get you to back off. Some things are said to trick you into thinking something that just isn't true, or to get you heading off in a wrong direction. Sometimes things are said with no deceptive intent whatsoever.

It is fairly natural to look for assurances that what we want to have happen is happening or will happen. You may want it enough that you hear things that aren't really said. This is something you can monitor. Remain alert to the fact that the more uncertain you become, the more vulnerable you will be to listening for what you want to hear.

Honest self-awareness helps a lot here. By keeping in touch with what it is you really want to hear, you can better test yourself to see if you are filtering some things out while mixing some things in. If you're not sure, it doesn't hurt to check with the source to confirm your perceptions. This is a good test anyway. If you are not comfortable doing so, that's probably a good sign that you are afraid of what you'll hear.

Be aware of whose interests you are protecting

Whom have we been trained to question? Who is not used to being directly questioned? What does that indicate to you about who is eligible for annoyance?

This question particularly applies to those of us who work in some capacity involving public service. We may be human services workers, city government staff, or educators, to name a few such positions. It is common to get identified with others who are engaged in the same or similar service. That's not a bad thing. We come to know each other, create a network of relationships, share information, and share a common outlook. But sometimes this gets in the way. It can interfere with our ability to have frank and needed discussions about actions that are needed to benefit the people we are supposed to be helping.

Over time, as we identify with our professional group, we may become far too separated from those we serve and assist, those who are truly supposed to benefit from our actions. We can become separated from their struggles and from their hopes. When the time comes to challenge the system we work for, we may have forgotten whose interests we are supposed to be serving.

We don't want to offend our colleagues by calling into question their actions or inactions. Subtle norms or codes of behavior creep in to keep us from squarely facing up to difficulties caused by those associates who are not fulfilling their responsibilities. We have rules of politeness. Yet adhering to these rules may be very impolite to those who must bear the consequences of incompetent or inadequate actions.

Confrontation of a colleague in the interest of those whom we serve, even if handled in a professional and polite manner, is far less common than it should be. (Behind the back sniping, though, is not uncommon enough.) We don't want to rock the boat. Basically, we don't want to rock our boats. What about those people whose boats are already dangerously rocking? Those people who are depending on us for constructive action? Well, they're used to it. They'll put up with the grief. Their turmoil is much more acceptable than the difficulty that could be created by challenging someone who works in the system that is supposed to be helping.

Direct, sustained confrontation of powerful people is also rare. This is particularly true when the potential target has some power over those who are feeling dissatisfied. This power provides a protective shield that causes those of us who may be angry or frustrated to back away. Maybe we read some sign that says, "Please do not disturb." So we don't.

You see, those people we are afraid to discomfort, for whom we don't really want to create any unpleasantness, are much more like us than the people we are supposed to serve. If we cannot fully work on behalf of those we are there to assist, but instead conjure up rationalizations for our own inactions, we have become the "them" that people talk about.

Avoid making excuses

Making excuses is one of the most unflattering things you can do. It implies that external forces that you can neither sufficiently comprehend nor take into account have more to do with your performance than you do. It says that you are unprepared to handle the unexpected.

Excuses lure you into a "can't do" mentality. You can easily get hooked on looking for reasons to explain why you aren't doing what you need to do. If this becomes a habit, you will end up not believing in yourself, and others will realize they can't count on you.

You probably don't like to hear excuses. They are as annoying as mosquitoes, and they sound as irritating coming from you as they do coming from anybody else. Making excuses ultimately involves asking others to treat you as if you are not responsible. It is probably more effective not to ask others to treat you that way and not to treat yourself that way either.

Occasionally, factors truly outside your control or reasonable anticipation will occur to prevent you from taking the action you intend. There may also be times when you are belittled for some shortcoming for which you are not responsible. This may be unwarranted, and you may need to defend yourself. In those cases you may simply ask, without attacking back, if an explanation is wanted. If one is wanted, you can offer it. If one is not, you have made your point, and there is probably little to be gained in complaining.

When you hear yourself fashioning an excuse in anticipation that you will need to offer one, let that be a signal unto you. You are probably trying to deal with how you feel about your actions or inactions rather than with what has or hasn't happened.

Accept that there will be a time or two when you mess up. We all do. Most of the time these are things we could have avoided or dealt with more effectively. Learn from the situation. Give less weight to obstacles and more to your own ability.

The moment you believe you are powerless you will indeed be powerless

None of us is truly powerless. We all possess some ability, some resources, some way to take or produce action. Surely, in each situation some people have more power, perhaps much more power, and others have less. Yet in no situation is anyone totally without power. Even people who have severe restrictions placed on their power, like prisoners or children, for example, have some ability to cause a reaction that they intend. When many people with little power combine their efforts like the many drops of water in a downpour, the accumulated power can have a remarkable effect.

Nobody can make you powerless but yourself. Ironically, powerlessness is also an exercise of power because you have chosen it yourself. If you believe you have no power, you will act that way, and your "powerlessness" will be true. If you believe you have some degree of power, even a very small amount, you will begin to see things that you can do.

Look forward to some dessert

I hated green beans as a kid. Still don't much like them. They seemed to accompany every other meal in our home when I was growing up. Probably an exaggeration, but such was my distaste that I feared they lurked in any innocent appearing pot. I got through the green beans by looking at the dessert on the counter. Dessert actually did accompany most meals. Knowing I had some pudding or cake or other tasty delight awaiting the completion of my basic dinner responsibilities kept me going through the green beans, beets, or any other drastically healthy item on my plate.

It still does. You see, life dishes out a lot of green beans. Boring, tedious responsibilities may seem to weigh down your days and weeks. It can be hard to get through all of that with a smile on your face, knowing that there are more green beans to come. So, put some dessert in your life. Give yourself fun and pleasant things to look forward to. A concert, a weekend fishing, a trip to another town—all these can brighten your view of the future and make the present more palatable. Smaller things can as well. Have dinner with a friend or take in a movie. You have lots of choices.

I firmly believe in having something to look forward to. It helps put the drudgery in its place, keeping it from taking up your life. And don't wait until everything is done (because it never will be) before you allow yourself to sit down to some dessert. Don't put your desserts too far off in the future, either. In fact, give yourself lots of them. It's the kind of thing that will keep you really healthy.

CHAPTER **5**

Ways to Approach Promoting Change

An effective change agent knows how to do things well. This is only one word different from knowing how to do things. That little difference is likely to be the difference between effectiveness and mediocrity. Things you may read in textbooks can give you important information on the process of change. Yet the subtle things that sustain the life of a change effort sometimes lie hidden between the lines. These Rules of the Game will help you make things work.

At first you may not see yourself as a change agent, giving fiery speeches and leading inspirational rallies. This is a common misperception of the change agent's role. A change agent keeps things in motion. If you can't give fiery speeches, find someone who can. A certain flair for motivational oratory comes in handy, but this talent is by and large secondary, and its effects are usually short lived. More important are the skills you have acquired that allow you to recognize the nuances of a situation and to conduct yourself accordingly. Effective change agents are more likely to be perceptive, creative, and determined than they are to be flamboyant.

It really is the fundamental attention you give to helping people believe in themselves, believe in each other, believe in the importance of the work, and do what needs to be done that matters most. Figuring out the outlines of the work, the strategies and tactics, is important, but less demanding.

How you look at a situation and your ability to adjust your responses are important talents. Keep asking yourself, "How do we make this work?" To answer that question you need to answer four others:

1. Given the situation we face and the resources we have, what is the right thing to do?

2. What do we need to do to get people doing the right things, in the right way, at the right time?
3. How can members learn and gain confidence in themselves to figure our these things on their own?
4. How do we keep all this together?

Some common themes are woven through many of the rules in this chapter. They play a part in increasing your effectiveness and in guiding your selection of specific tactics. They are present in the way you go about engaging resistance or developing support. You will see that they contribute to your approach to developing the strength of your organization. Let's look at these themes individually before tackling these Rules of the Game.

Any approach you take to promoting change must start with a clear decision to act.   First, you must clearly decide to act; generally this requires some degree of risk taking. Further, when every action is directed by a clear, intended outcome, you can focus your work much more effectively. Most change efforts, especially in the early stages, do not have an overabundance of power. Therefore, you give yourself a much greater chance for success when your power is clearly focused on a particular outcome.

Your approaches to promoting change are built around an issue that participants can rally around.   The issue provides the change effort's reason for being. An action-oriented issue provides both the clarity of focus and the spark for action that every change effort needs. A good issue will continue to attract attention and participation.

Approaches to promoting change require that you make conscious choices.   Use yourself and the organization purposefully. Keep yourselves committed to doing what works, and get things done. Leave to chance only those things that don't matter or those about which you can do nothing.

The approaches you decide to take will be aided by a frequent analysis of the situation.   The process of change is a dynamic one. Analyze the various forces at play, the emerging opportunities, the patterns of responses, and, especially, the progress you are making. Your choices have a predictive quality; that is, the actions you take are geared to an outcome you can predict. It becomes important then that you anticipate what is likely to occur, including the fact that you cannot anticipate everything.

Approaches to promoting change generally produce countermovement or resistance. A change agent needs to recognize the opposition and gauge it accurately. To counter or reduce opposition, an effective change agent will anticipate both the likelihood of opposition and its sources. When a change agent can reduce the degree of opposition, the organization will conserve energy that can be directed toward building support. Look for the avenue in each situation that provides the least resistance. Some opponents can be turned into allies, or at least neutralized, and not all opponents need to be fought. Though there are occasions when a change agent may want to precipitate a conflict, this should be a conscious, strategic decision. Avoid creating unnecessary opposition.

Approaches to dealing with opposition should be thoughtfully developed. Assess both the nature and strength of the opponent and the capability of your base of support. It is fairly common for those trying to make a change to consider the strength of the opponent or the size of the challenge while forgetting their own strengths. You will benefit from honestly recognizing and using your own strengths.

The approaches you use are necessarily built on the depth and extent of your support and the variety of options this support gives you. It is important to recognize actual and potential support, develop it, and gauge it accurately. Your work is aided by the growth of an organized group. Depending on the nature of the change you are pursuing, your organization will vary in size, from a handful of people to even thousands.

The approaches you undertake must strengthen the ways members of the organization relate to each other and to the action agenda. Look for opportunities to promote broad investment in the effort. Spreading the work around and increasing opportunities for leadership and decision making helps participants feel more connected to the effort. Filling key roles within the organization promotes harmony and helps the group accomplish its goals. Knowing that internal malaise and dissension defeat more change efforts than do external enemies should remind you to pay attention to these matters.

Approaches to change that make use of creativity and the unexpected can add life to the effort. After an initial burst of enthusiasm, things can begin to drag. Actions that stir excitement and interest sustain momentum. There is a further benefit. Your ability to remain unpredictable keeps opponents off balance.

The approaches you use either to build support or to deal with oppo-sition must take into account how people actually relate to the world. Depending on their values, experiences, and general reference points, people notice different things. These same factors influence how they react as well. To get any reaction at all, you must first get their attention. To develop successful strategies, you must see the situation through their eyes.

The rules in this chapter offer some guidance in how to approach this business of change. They will help you develop your own framework for viewing a change opportunity and for promoting effectively organized action. It is these basic notions, not the fancy ones, that give you the critical edge that so many seem to miss. Pay attention to the rules as you begin to do what needs to be done to make a difference.

Improving Your Effectiveness

The first set of rules in this chapter provides some simple ways to make your actions more productive. Seemingly minor adjustments to your approach may produce major benefits.

If you don't know where you're going,
you probably won't get there

You are all loaded into the car. The kids are securely fastened in the back seat. Over the next several hours you will have the opportunity to turn your attention from the front of the car to the rear and ask, "What's going on back there?" in a voice that says you don't really want an answer. You are going to visit Aunt Irsle in Biloxi, and it's going to be *fun!*

You have a clear goal in mind. As you start out, you may not know all the roads you'll need to take, much less just where all the turns, exits, and detours will be. You may have a flat tire or other automotive setback to slow you down along the way. You may have to deal with the inevitable milkshake all over the floor incident. But you know where you are headed, and you are determined to get there.

Compare that with some of the change efforts you may have been involved in. They start out with the idea that "we're going to make things better," and they don't seem to evolve much beyond that point. You may not even discuss just what "better" looks like, let alone agree to it. In fact, what "better" looks like may depend on who you are talking to. It's somewhat like jumping in the car to go on a family trip with everyone having their own idea about where you are heading.

I am frequently asked to assist groups who seem to be floundering. In such cases I ask the members to individually write down in one sentence just what the goal of the group is (or what they intend to accomplish in the next six months). For a moment everyone looks a little lost. Then members glance at one another, apparently hoping to get some sign, and sheepishly scribble a few words. The point is made. We don't even have to read all the various "goals" floating around in the group— but it is kind of fun to do, and it breaks up the tension.

Groups such as these end up spending a lot of energy going sideways. They don't move forward. No one seems quite sure what to do. It is not uncommon for these groups to start arguing among themselves. Members criticize each other (often indirectly) for taking the wrong action or no action at all. Without a clear sense of direction it is hard to commit to any particular action, and it is next to impossible to figure out just what the right action might be. Those who feel frustrated by a lack of direction usually either drop out or take over, forcing their goals on the rest of the group. This may make a few people relieved, a few resentful, and may even cause some others to quit.

You don't need a clear picture of your goals to bring people together, but you do need a definite sense of direction once people begin working. Confidence comes with knowing where you are headed. This is a much different feeling than you have when you don't know where you want to go or when you feel lost. Knowing what you want to accomplish provides a focus to your efforts and helps you discover one of the most difficult places in your journey—the starting point. Knowing clearly what outcome you are trying to produce or what "better" looks like will keep you going past the detours and the flat tires. Enjoy the trip.

Ask forgiveness, not permission

This is a favorite saying of my friend, Punch Woods, an accomplished organizer and administrator. This philosophy has enabled people like Punch to move forward while others put self-evident plans on delay, seeking the approval from someone who probably isn't directly involved in the matter anyway.

Whoa, there. Isn't that a bit reckless, just busting ahead and ignoring the consequences? Yes, it can be. Certainly, ignoring consequences would be foolish. It is possible to produce a short-term gain but generate a long-term loss. In actual practice it is pretty hard to punish someone for success, but deciding not to ask permission should be done with some thoughtfulness.

In many cases, the energy of the moment can wither and an immediate opportunity can be lost as you pursue a series of burdensome steps to get approval for your action. Appointments must be arranged, a case presented, discussion held, and a little time set aside to "think it over." Maybe your question will be referred to yet another person, and the dance must repeated with another partner. Is all this necessary? Sometimes, yes. If that is true, your effort may be harmed if you ignore that fact. However, often the answer is no. All that tripping around may not be necessary.

We get back again to the notion of discipline. There is at least a little arrogance involved in deciding that you can act without permission from those who have the authority to grant it and the expectation to be asked. It can be slightly heady to take on that authority yourself. An effective change agent does have a bit of impertinence. After all, the change agent has enough audacity to challenge the status quo. However, it is important to temper that arrogance with discipline. Keep the interest of the change effort in the forefront, and consult this mental checklist to determine whether you should act or wait.

1. Do you really need permission to act? Is it possible that your group is seeking confirmation rather than permission? You may be unsure of yourselves and looking for someone to tell you that you're on the right track. Perhaps you're looking for someone who will bear the responsibility in case things don't work out.
2. Whose permission do you think you need? Is this person a likely ally who would probably support the action anyway? Is this a person whose likely refusal you could circumvent by action? Will this person bear a grudge, and will that matter down the road? Is it important to give this authority some control over what your group can decide? Does your action commit someone to do something without their permission to do so? Does this person really see themselves as needing to grant permission?
3. What are the likely consequences? Are they major or minor? Most of the time you will get some sort of lecture and slap on the wrist in exchange for your "sorry, I won't do that again." In those cases the cost is worth it. Sometimes, the reaction is more serious. Whatever the consequences, you must be aware of them before you act and be prepared to handle them if they occur. But remember that not acting also has consequences.

This sounds highly rational, like some sort of math equation. It's not. It involves some educated guesses and an element of risk taking. Some situations are clearer than others. You are the best judge of how important the likely actions and reactions are. The need to ask presumes a course of action that is at least outside the routine, if not very different. However, the easy answer to your asking is no. Given that I believe in the principle of "ask forgiveness, not permission," my orientation is, when in doubt, act.

Don't ask, "Can we?" Ask, "How can we?"

If you do decide to ask for permission, you may increase your chances for a favorable result simply by the way you ask. Asking "Can we?" puts you at a disadvantage. Decision making has been taken completely out of your hands and given to another who may not have the same interest and information you have. You can hardly give away the right to make a decision and then ask for it back if you don't like the answer. To avoid this pitfall, ask "*How* can we?" This leads to more promising possibilities. The question itself implies a level of agreement. You have put the conversation on a different plane by shifting the focus to implementation. You have become partners in problem solving. The question of permission becomes secondary to the question of strategy. Further, though you have opened the possibility of rejection of your proposal, you haven't given away your right to discuss it.

If people agree, your best strategy is to shut up

It had taken many months of maneuvering. Attack was met with counterattack, sometimes subtle, sometimes not. They had finally reached an agreement. Some were happy. They had more or less gotten what they wanted. Others were not. They felt they had acquiesced more than they had agreed. There was some sense of relief, but not enough to cleanse the room of the tension that still clung so tightly to the participants.

The awkward silence was broken by Ken, "I knew you would eventually see things our way. Now that you have agreed, we can go ahead with our plans to . . ." He finished by leaning back in his chair looking contented, if not smug, having detailed all that the agreement could mean.

Looking like she'd been slapped, Terry snapped back. "You can what!? This agreement is not about all your plans to. . . . Maybe we need to rethink this."

The agreement had involved a specific number of items that had been in dispute. It was not intended to authorize all the "plans" either group had in mind. Now was not the time to rub people's noses in matters that were not directly a part of the agreement, matters they may not like and were certainly not prepared to support. It may be a long next few months.

I have seen agreements undone by supporters too enthusiastic or relieved to have the good sense to be quiet. They can't seem to stop gushing about what the agreement means to them. It is a rather one-sided dialogue that unwittingly acknowledges only one set of interests and can easily dredge up conflicts not wholly healed. Rambling on can be enough to undermine a newly formed agreement. You can clarify what the agreement is without speculating about all that it may (or may not) mean.

Sometimes agreements among parties in an uncertain, newly formed relationship require some sensitivity as well. At the time of the agreement avoid talking about what it proves or speculating about untested implications. Simply accept the fact that an agreement has occurred and that the responsibilities of each party are clear. If you need to discuss anything at all, discuss the next step the parties will take. Agreements become real when they are acted on; it is wise to begin implementing the agreement soon.

Follow up and follow through

On many occasions you may request action from people outside your organization. Perhaps this individual is a city council member who will put together some funding package for you. Maybe you need help from a political confidant who will pursue inquiries for you. Or, you may have asked officials in another organization to make arrangements for you to meet with other community leaders.

Though you place some responsibility in the hands of these other individuals, you cannot completely let it go. Even if they have a high degree of support for your cause, they have a higher degree of support for their own interests. Agreements can be forgotten, put temporarily aside, or changed in the face of the competing demands of their own affairs. You will need to devise some method for staying on top of the situation.

Normally your follow-up can be built into your initial agreement. "When should I check back with you?" or "Should I give you a call next week to see how things are going?" is usually sufficient. The important thing is to agree on when and how you may recontact the other party. Otherwise you may end up bugging the other person and be seen as a pest. Your follow-up provides a sort of deadline that keeps the agreement current.

Doing your part to follow through is important as well. When working with others, each party has responsibilities. Each of you, to some extent, depends on the other's performance. On some occasions you will be called on to complete work started by others. At other times, requests will be made of you by an ally. Your ability to fulfill commitments will solidify important relationships and establish you as a credible partner. Also, it will demonstrate how you expect to be treated.

These matters—following up and following through—seem so simple and obvious that you may wonder if they are worth mentioning. Believe me, they are. Inattention to these two things is a major factor that causes change efforts to stall or fail. Most change efforts will have some success and will achieve success more quickly, with less frustration, if you follow up and follow through. It is not a lack of good ideas that kills off most change efforts, it's the lack of acting on the good ideas we have.

Pay attention to details

What ever happened to "don't sweat the small stuff?" That's still pretty good advice. Small stuff includes those things over which you do not have control and those things that really don't matter in the scheme of things. Those things may well be different from "details." Details are those little things that do mean something. They often represent the difference between a little success and a lot more success.

Details are those finishing touches that make an activity complete. Without them, things are not finished or not as well done. They are the sign-in sheet passed around at a presentation done by your group. They are parking spaces for the news crews attending your news conference. They are making certain that someone is prepared to be interviewed when someone from the local station shows up at the site you are picketing. They are the clear directions printed for each person going door-to-door in your neighborhood, so they know where they are going and what they are going to say when someone opens the door. They are "makeing shure their ar no errers in youre grups' literture."

Make the most out of every opportunity. Whenever your group makes contact with the public, you have an opportunity to attract new supporters for your cause. You can leave with names, addresses, and phone numbers, or you could just leave with a good feeling from the warm reception. Which do you think will help more?

Your attention to details helps to shape how you see yourselves and how others see you. It affects your credibility. Does all your printed material have a union bug? If not, why not? Does your letterhead look like you are to be taken seriously? Do you know what questions to ask when you call the mayor's office? Do you have the facts at hand that you need? Do you appear to be sloppy or organized in what you do? In what little ways can you represent yourselves more effectively? Much of this doesn't require extra work so much as a little extra attention. You don't need to be fancy, but it does help to be thorough.

Anticipate, anticipate, anticipate. Take just 5 minutes to review any planned event or task to see if there is anything missing. For every activity, see if you can guess what is likely to happen and how you will respond. Do you have the things in place that you need? Recognizing the little pieces of the puzzle helps you prevent problems and get the most out of each situation.

Use good judgment in deciding how to approach different types of activities. Some activities are marked more by their spontaneous quality than by their total organization. You probably don't have to plan a potluck down to the last detail, but it might be nice to have enough forks for everyone. Learn the difference between the little things that don't matter and the little ones that do.

Never assume that your interests are unimportant to important people

"We can't ask him, he's important." They looked at me expectantly, waiting for me to come to my senses and realize what a dumb idea I had suggested. Or maybe they were hoping I'd let them off the hook, tell them that's OK, we can just keep talking to ourselves. I looked back, waiting too. My answer didn't take them off the hook. "And you are?" I asked back.

We tend to make up things about people we don't know, people who are different from us. Those of us who see ourselves as unimportant make up things about people whom we see as important. There is some degree of truth in these things we imagine, but there is fiction as well.

Our failure to approach people who may have greater status and influence than we may say as much about us as it does about them. It is not comfortable to go outside one's group, regardless of what group that might be. However, unless your group has all the resources it needs, you will not accomplish your goals without reaching beyond your circle.

Important people, or a particular important person, may or may not be willing to assist you. You will never know unless you make a request.

Keeping your issues and yourselves separate from or unknown to others, important or not, keeps them from acting to help. Important people are just like anybody else, distracted with their own interests or worries. Like anyone else, they can be ignorant of what other people need. This does not mean they are incapable of recognizing need and acting on that recognition.

True, some people aren't going to consider your issues important, and they won't lift a finger to help you. Yes, this is true about some important people. So what? It is true about people who have little social status as well. Are you more afraid of not getting a favorable response from someone you believe to be important than from someone you don't believe to be important? Will you feel worse? If so, there may be some learning for you there.

Just like anyone else, some important people are more likely to help than others. If there is something in particular you need—a political favor, a public statement, a thousand dollars—do a little homework on who is more likely to help and decide how each person could be approached.

When you do ask for assistance, ask in the spirit of collaboration. With your time, information, and dedication, you are an important contributor to success, not a hat-holding supplicant. The people you are asking assistance from have important contributions to make as well. They are your partners, not your superiors.

All people can be seen as potential contributors. I have seen so-called important people come to care very deeply about issues that more directly affect those seen as less important. I have seen them moved from ignorance to awareness to action. I have seen their help matter.

You are worth it. What you care about is important. The basic methods for reaching out to important people are the same as you would use with anyone else. You target those most likely to respond to you, you invite with a purposeful request, and you follow up to maintain support.

Get your facts straight

Information is a source of power. It clarifies the situation you are facing. It creates interest and can evoke emotion. It provides direction for action. It better be accurate.

Your understanding of an issue, and your intent to do something about it, stems from information, from facts. Facts give the issue shape and meaning. They create outrage, excitement, hope, and urgency. Facts pinpoint those things that exist in the situation that you must change. They show you what obstructs progress and what you can use. They tell you what is wrong and what is possible. Facts can be hard data, particular incidents, or concrete examples. They are real and reliable.

Rumor is not fact. Neither is what "everyone knows." There may be facts hidden there, but you'll find a lot of imagination as well. When we are dissatisfied about a situation, we tend to create information that meets our dissatisfaction. The more we say and hear something, the more it becomes "true," even if it's not. If your information is faulty, your grasp of the issue is weakened. As a result, your approach may be haphazard and your direction unclear or wrong. So, don't pretend. Get the facts. Inaccurate information leaves you vulnerable both to miscalculation and to embarrassment

Imagine that you are going on a long hike. Your backpack is all loaded, your boots are laced up, and you've got your trail map and compass. Funny thing about that trail map, though, the distances between key points are wrong. The names for some of the trails aren't right either, and some have been left off altogether. You are going to spend a lot of time wandering around. If you don't get lost, you may just give up and go home.

Your journey to promote change can be much like that hike. Your decisions about the nature of the challenge, as well as your assessment of allies, opponents, and those who are just disinterested will direct the steps you will take. If you miss some essential points here and there or have some erroneous information, you can spend a lot of time wandering around before you give up and go home.

Yes, misdirection may be a problem but so, too, may be the loss of believability. Here's another scene to imagine. You are in a packed meeting room with city officials, police, some in uniform and some in ties, neighbors, mothers, fathers, old people and young. You are going to get this community policing issue straightened out. Your neighborhood is being neglected, and you are not going to put up with this any longer. Neglect is the issue, pure and simple—never checked your facts though. Your neighborhood has more cops per capita than almost all neighborhoods in the city. A higher percentage of the police budget is spent in your precinct than in the areas you have cited as receiving preferential treatment. Response time is above average for all neighborhoods, and the prevention efforts you say are lacking really did start a month ago. A little late to say, "Oops. Never mind." How many people will be at the next meeting you call?

Your sense of frustration may be legitimate, but you had better be clear about what that discontent is based on, especially if facts are available to support or question your case. A challenge to the status quo generally needs to meet higher tests of accuracy than does preservation of the status quo. Your ability to cite clear facts will keep people from avoiding the issue and will rivet attention on the matters that concern you. They give you a reference point to keep issues in focus. If you do not know what you are talking about, it will be hard to get people to listen. It will be next to impossible to promote constructive action.

You know somebody who kind of shoots off at the mouth, whose information is more than a little bit suspect, who, let's say, is given to exaggerating a bit. I bet you can name that person. How much do you rely on what that individual has to say? People of this sort may come to believe what they are saying, and they may even believe that you believe them. You don't.

Organizations and people who lead them can have such a reputation. After a while no one really takes them seriously, and they are pretty easy to discredit. You want your issue to be taken seriously, so don't let this happen to you.

We all tend to listen to "facts" that confirm our positions, and we tend to ignore those that don't. That is natural, but in the arena of community change, it is sloppy. Be willing to question the authenticity of your information. Rest assured that if you don't someone else will.

When you know what you are talking about, you feel stronger. You can assert yourself more and listen better to opposition. Clear and accurate information also provides legitimacy. It allows people to believe in the organization and to trust it with their time and hope. If offered well, it demands recognition. It makes things real.

Getting your facts straight is a fundamental starting point. This is not something you can get to later. You will never know everything there is to know about your issue and your situation, but be sure that what you do know is accurate and reliable. Your command of information will strengthen you with confidence and credibility, two essential elements for taking action and building support.

Don't just think about doing things, do them

Pick up the phone and make the call instead of writing it down on your list of things to do. Much of the burden of taking action is the thought of all the action that must be taken. Doing something is a lot less strenuous than carrying around the worry of having it to do.

Taken together everything you must do may be a lot, but you don't have to do it all at once. Don't wait for that 4-hour block of time when you can "just concentrate" on the things you need to do. It ain't gonna come. You don't need to complete a task at one sitting; it may be enough just to start it. Taking a little bit of action tends to energize and even lead to a little more action. You end up feeling that things are a little more manageable, and you don't feel so overwhelmed. You will even notice progress.

Meetings often turn into "What should we do?" conversations: "We need to call Joe and ask him to review the agreement. We need to call Mary and ask her if she met with the people from City Planning." And so on, you get the picture. In a 10-minute conversation you can come up with a lot of "to do's." People leave the meeting burdened with still more of their life undone. Know what works for me? Do them right there on the spot. We need to call Joe? Let's call him. I pick up the phone and dial. This seems to surprise people, but in a 10-minute period you can come up with a lot of "done's."

If you are enjoying whatever it is you are doing, keep doing it. If, however, you are fretting about what you should be doing, that's a different thing. Unless you are otherwise engaged in something important, like having dinner with your lover or playing with your children, when you catch yourself thinking about something you need to do, start doing it.

Observe the rule of the final inch

Almost done is not done. The journey is not complete until the last inch has been traversed, observed Alexander Solzhenitsyn. This is true for your change effort too.

Often, just before the thing is complete, people let up. They let go of their hold on things and allow inertia and the flow of events to take over. There is a moment of permanent surrender to the whisper of close enough.

"C'mon, we've got it pretty well planned out. Let's go home. We can get together 10 minutes before the meeting starts and finish things up then." Last night's conversation. We were preparing to meet the next day with representatives of the group we'd been battling to finally get things settled. The effort to get there 10 minutes ahead of time and do that last little bit of planning proved to be too much.

Now we have figured out what we didn't quite figure out before. Now we know how to end the meeting, to bring things to a close that would have given us what we had been working these last five months to get. Now the meeting is over, and we let it slip away.

I was at that meeting. I knew we had lost our chance. After five months of work, almost half a year, why couldn't we go for 10 more minutes? I had this sick, smoldering feeling that I didn't ever want to have again.

Since that time I have recognized how curiously easy it is to stop working when the work should be at its easiest, when it is almost done. When you are almost to that point you have struggled so hard to get to, it is difficult to summon the energy to push through that invisible wall between you and done. With the final inch untraveled, whatever you were working on remains unfinished, incomplete, even if it has now become some tiny part of history. The meeting you had almost finished planning—now it's over and done with. The position paper still awaiting its refinements—now it's printed and distributed. The final details of the agreement you worked so hard to achieve—now you just assume it is intact.

So what is this final inch? Is it perfection? Must you not rest until perfection has been achieved? No, that would be ridiculous and impossible. The final inch is reached when you have done the best you can do, given your circumstances, to take care of every important piece of your task that needs to be done. Otherwise, whatever you let fill in that last little space, you leave up to luck or to some others' interests.

The final inch may be mysteriously difficult to cross, but it may be the most important inch you travel. In some way it will count. Doing the best you can do will more than likely lead to something better than if you did something less. Close to where you want to be is a different place from where you want to be.

Tactical Considerations

This set of rules covers questions of tactics, including the principles behind the maneuvers you can take to create an advantage for your group. In most cases groups organizing for change have little initial power or credibility. These rules will help you get the most out of what you have.

Use appropriate channels

Use appropriate channels—this rule usually meets with less than enthusiastic reception. The reaction goes something like this. "Let me see if I've got this straight. We are set to pursue a change in an organization that needs it, and we are relying on their 'appropriate channels' to accept the change. Have you been out in the sun too long?"

OK, so there's normally a little resistance. Change agents don't like to entrust their ideas to those who may turn out to be the opposition, especially when the keepers of those "appropriate channels" commonly have more power than those seeking the change. Also, the caretakers of the appropriate channels commonly have some vested interest in keeping things the way they are. They are reluctant to accept change. So, why should you rely on their vested interests and power, not yours?

You don't. You *use* the appropriate channels, you don't *rely* on them. There are a number of reasons why this rule makes good sense, but first I'd better explain what I mean about using but not relying.

Using the appropriate channels is one course of action you take, but not the only one. From the very beginning you prepare a series of actions to take if the system does not respond in a timely manner. This gives you another set of tactics in reserve. Prepare a backup plan to put in place in the somewhat likely event that the appropriate channels don't work. Don't wait until you recognize the failure of the system before planning alternative actions. (A fact that is sometimes helpful to "leak" to your opponent.) Prepare in advance, and decide how much time is reasonable for the proposed change to make its way through the system. This time line establishes when you can declare the process a failure.

In effect, you are operating on two different levels. The first level is the public one of following procedures. The second is a private one, your backup plan, the alternative actions you will take if progress at the first level is much too slow or nonexistent.

Once it is clear that proper channels prevent rather than promote improvement, you can begin to implement your reserve plan. Often it is helpful to make the lack of responsiveness an issue itself. This creates a situation in which the resisting party must either prove you wrong by becoming responsive or prove you right by continuing their resistance. You can demonstrate that you have acted in good faith, where they have not. You can show that you took a cooperative stance, whereas they continued in arrogance or insensitivity.

Those who are already committed to your cause will intensify their resolve, and those who have not yet taken a position may move in your direction. The uncommitted may well grant powerful interests an initial benefit of the doubt, but they still remain suspicious. When suspicions of contempt for the less powerful are confirmed, you stand to strengthen the support you have and gain a number of allies who will find it hard to ignore the reality they may have suspected all along.

To reap the benefit of this tactic, you need to present it in a way that decision makers, supporters, and potential allies notice. That's the whole point. You are creating a perception of your issue and how it relates to those who have some authority, and you are creating a perception of how those in authority relate to your issue and the people it affects. In the meantime you can apply subtle internal and external pressure on the system to help make the channels work. In so doing, you are taking steps within your control.

Why go through all this hassle? Why not just start with your backup plan to begin with? Because you want to be effective, not just in a hurry.

There are several reasons for using appropriate channels, even if you do not rely on them. First, they may work. Second, by not following procedures you give the target system an excuse for not dealing with you. The system can easily represent itself as the victim of an ill-informed, if not insolent, group. You don't want them saying, "We have procedures in place for dealing with these concerns, but your group either didn't take the time to find out about them or doesn't care to." Such a response may be generally accepted by less involved members of the community, which may be most of the community. Then you will have to do extra work to regain their support.

Third, when you are confronting the status quo, you are somewhat of an irritant. Especially early on when your base of support is likely to be small, you may be seen as more of a bother than anything else. Though the public may have some questions, an aura of legitimacy surrounds the actions of powerful interests, including powerful organizations, such as city governments, religious organizations, or universities. Their positions and approaches to handling questions are generally accepted as being valid, and it is usually up to those who challenge such interests to first prove their reasonableness. There is a certain decorum and rationality to following proper procedures, which serves to protect against upset. Even though it may not be true, most people want to pretend that the boat is steady, that the captain is thoughtfully steering a true course. They aren't so comfortable with those who rock the boat. It makes them nervous. Ignoring the proper procedures may lead to unwelcome upset for the uncommitted both inside and outside the target system. These potential supporters may come to disapprove of your actions and your concerns. It is almost as if we are all supposed to play this game, even if we don't like it. Some may even say, "Who the heck are you to think these rules don't apply to you?" The shift in opposition may be subtle, but it is an added weight you'll have to handle.

Fourth, by taking the appropriate steps you can clearly demonstrate that you have acted in good faith, but that the procedures just don't work. You can show that the target is insensitive, arrogant, or incompetent in dealing with your legitimate issues. Your group's ideas become the alternative to an ineffective system. The target is now on the defensive.

So, by using the appropriate channels you put the ball in their court, you force them to respond. You avoid alienating those who are as yet uncommitted. You stay on top of the situation and hold the system accountable, increasing expectations and mounting pressure. Meanwhile, you gear up to pursue other tactics once you can show that the channels don't work. You create the opportunity for the system to respond properly, but you rely on your own actions to move the process forward.

An exception to this approach can be made when you initially have a significant amount of power in the given situation. In that case, you may go straight to the heart of the matter, bypassing the tedious pursuit of proper channels. By being direct you demonstrate your authority. To do otherwise risks giving your power away to a labyrinth of stops and starts that can drain your energy and advantage.

Hold people accountable, and keep the pressure on

Although you should always hold people accountable, the degree of pressure required to achieve your goal is related to the degree of resistance you encounter. You don't need to give a hard time to people who are ready to cooperate with you.

You may hear more promises made than you see kept. A common tactic for powerful groups that are under some pressure is to make insincere promises or statements that sound good but have little substance. Pin them down on the substance. Clear, observable measures of performance are necessary for accountability. This includes time lines, standards of quality, amount of money to be provided, or specific actions to be taken. Verbal agreements should be confirmed in writing.

One way of increasing the pressure a bit is to discuss with the other party what actions should be taken if measures of performance are not met. For example, if something is to be done by a certain date, it is useful to talk in advance about what steps should be taken if the date is missed. It is more important to demonstrate the seriousness of your purpose than the seriousness of your desire to hassle.

You need to immediately recognize when a measure is met or missed. When it is met, take time to acknowledge that things went well. This can be done by a phone call or letter or by public recognition, such as an award, when appropriate. When an agreement has not been fulfilled, it is important to call attention to the fact at once by inquiring into the situation. Making contact prior to the completion date of an agreed-upon action conveys your attentiveness to the situation and confirms the importance of the agreement. You may want to allow a little margin, giving the other party a chance to complete their responsibilities before you invoke any sanction. This is generally a good idea because it allows for movement toward more collaborative relationships, which are more productive than combative ones. However, there are occasions when an immediate sanction is necessary.

Pressure is usually brought by increasing the frequency of contact, increasing the number of sources making a contact, increasing the number of people who have to respond for the other party, increasing the public attention to the matter, and increasing the costs for violations. These approaches essentially involve two components: (1) drawing and keeping attention on the situation, and (2) making it more uncomfortable for the other party to ignore agreements than to meet them. Tactics may move from merely annoying to explicitly damaging.

The more personal and direct the contact the better. A face-to-face conversation is better than a phone call, which is better than an E-mail, and so on. Even if the other party ignores your phone calls, the messages pile up. It is not enough just to complain. While in each contact you express your dissatisfaction with the lack of helpful response, you also describe what a satisfying or helpful response looks like. With every contact you make you suggest a date for the next contact, with the time between contacts becoming shorter.

Sometimes you need to get others involved. You can even ask those resisting you who this might be. For example, you might say, "It doesn't look like my calls are making much difference. Who else should be calling you to get things moving?" Of course, they aren't going to tell you, but you have served notice that you are willing to bring others into the matter. Do have people lined up in advance before you use this ploy. These might be clients, members of the board of directors, legislators, or others who have a legitimate interest in the matter. The more significant these other individuals are to the resister, the better. Get numbers if you can't get significance. That is, if you can't get important people to call, get a lot of people to call.

By expanding the number of people you contact within the other party's organization—secretaries, colleagues, supervisors—you begin to increase pressure closer to home. If this still doesn't do the trick, make a public issue of it. Here, the public may not mean the general public but rather any other members of the community that is the scene of the brewing conflict—for example, all the employees of a university, the general membership of a religious denomination, or constituents of a professional organization. Of course, you may also focus the attention of the general public if the issue has some common broader reach. There are scores of ways to bring about this sort of attention—public demonstrations, picketing, use of the news media. When you involve more people within the other party's organization, you are drawing the pressure in tighter and tighter. When you involve more of the public, you are expanding the circle of attention.

You can target an individual for public attention or target the organization itself. You can also use misgivings about the entity to conjure up images of perfidy that are in keeping with the public's skepticism of powerful institutions. Understand that whatever public posturing you may do it is ultimately the actions of individual people that count.

Finally, you may consider invoking other costs for violation. These could include lawsuits, boycotts, loss of employment, or other sanctions that raise the cost of resistance to a point that is unacceptably high. You will probably be asked to back off in exchange for some agreement. Don't. You can back off in exchange to some action, but don't turn down the pressure until significant action is taken. Be sure your agreement is never greater than the importance of the action taken.

Push the discomfort upward

Unpleasant things have a way of flowing downhill. This occurs in all kinds of communities. Those in positions of power tend to make decisions or institute policies that create much more inconvenience for other people than for the decision makers. Perhaps the result of ignorance or perhaps arrogance, it is very common that decisions confirm the convenience and control of those in authority.

You are sitting in your office and a memo lands on your desk—new duties, more work, more stuff to weigh down your desk and your shoulders. If you are like most workers, you take a break . . . to find someone to grumble with. You talk about those "idiots in administration." Convinced of your own moral and intellectual rectitude, you set about the business of scrambling around trying to fit new demands into crowded hours. You fume. You fuss. You might mutter an unchurchlike word or two. You get ready to start yet another new pile, and in so doing you seal your own fate. As long as you are willing to accept the inconvenience yourself, it will be given to you. By protecting those in authority from feeling the uncomfortable consequences of their decisions and actions, you maintain the situation you curse. Push it back.

Don't grumble with your colleague, strategize. As with most things, it is unlikely that you can pursue this approach alone. To create a new routine, a good percentage of people at your level must routinely respond in the same way. Taking some time to develop a simple strategy is worthwhile. You want your responses to be clear, consistent, and relevant to the situation. What you might do in your office will be different from what you might do in your neighborhood. Yet in most situations there will be some fairly simple and safe way to pass the hassle back, if you take a little time to figure out what that might be.

This orientation will work for big problems or little irritants. It has particular value for those situations in which there is a hierarchy of authority, like a bureaucracy. Understand that the bigger and more far reaching the problem, the more energy and organization will be required.

It is usually more effective to pick one of two basic strategies: (1) bother people with more authority who are easily within reach, or (2) bother one person who can make a difference. With the first strategy you don't always have to go all the way to the top. That may be too far to push. Just go up one level. Take something off your desk, and put it on someone else's—someone who gets paid more than you do. (Remember, this is part of a purposeful strategy. You cannot do it alone.) In due time the people sitting at those desks will get as tired of getting things passed up to them as you are of things getting passed down to you. Simply passing the discomfort down won't work for them anymore because you have learned to pass the discomfort up. When you bump the discomfort up one level, a new set of people become part of the group of the disaffected, who increase the bumping up until enough people with enough authority are sufficiently uncomfortable or threatened with discomfort. This may take some time, but it doesn't take much intensity or involve much risk.

If you decide that those at the top of the ladder can be effectively reached by those who seem to be losing out, you are usually better served if you concentrate your strength on one individual. Focus your attention on one key person whose change of heart can change the situation. This keeps your energy from being spread farther than it can go. This approach may yield quicker results, but they may not be long lasting. Also, it tends to be riskier, requiring tightly orchestrated tactics.

This ritual of creating discomfort for those with less power is not restricted to office communities. Degrees of political disenfranchisement occur in all settings: neighborhoods written off by city officials, women discounted by health care providers, seriously mentally ill citizens ignored and endangered by the good people who fund wars. People with power are usually few in number and more routinely in contact with each other. Their power is usually easier to organize and solidify, thus they can more easily spread their whims and wills on the greater numbers who do not have the advantages of position, routine contact, or structural authority on their side.

Several advantages are held by those who have less formal power. First, you can act in nonroutine ways. Pushing up discomfort is one of those nonroutine ways, a circumstance for which those "above" may be unprepared. Another related tactic is organized noncompliance; that is, no one performs the behavior that those with more power have required. Also, you can use your position. From among the various positions you hold—taxpayer, caseworker, congregation member—select any particular requirements or unique authority associated with that position that can strengthen you. Finally, you can add to this the benefit of sheer numbers. A combination of these approaches can provide for many creative responses to the situation you face.

Be willing to do the unexpected

> I'm a tamale
> Shredded meat.
> Only a dollar
> Can't be beat.

And that's just the first verse. A tamale song. It was one of the corniest things I'd heard. (Pardon the pun, *masa* lovers.) Instead of an announcement in class about selling tamales for a student association fund-raiser, each class got a song. By the end of the day people were singing the tamale ditty in the hallways, and the tamales had all been sold by noon.

The room was set up in a huge rectangle of tables. On one end sat the seven members of the administration's hastily assembled appeals committee, faces done up in an assortment of scowls, puckers, and pure boredom. Draping a bit over the "top" of the rectangle along the sides sat some additional staff to serve the committee. Clear on the other end of the room, a fairly large room, sat the four representatives of those challenging an administrative policy. The chasm between the two groups was, oh, so wide. Guess who set up the room. Just before the hearing was to begin, the four members moved aside one of the tables, walked inside the forbidding rectangle, and sat right on the other side of the committee's table, faces and voices now a mere 3 feet apart. "Now we can begin," said one of the representatives. This totally flummoxed the committee. The tables had literally been turned.

The predictability of patterns of behavior can keep us from seeing things. They certainly can keep us from changing direction or from establishing new patterns of behavior. They may manage our attention, they do not attract our attention. Predictable patterns may be used to re-inforce relative positions of power between groups, to stifle conflict, to keep unwanted information from coming to our attention, or simply to disregard those things that distract from the pursuit of immediate mat-ters. In short, predictable patterns guard against the new, the unknown, and maintain the status quo.

By doing the expected you reinforce prevailing methods and their likely results. By doing the unexpected you throw things out of balance, a little out of whack. Those involved may then come to look at the situa-tion in a whole new way. You help make us notice.

This does take a degree of spunk. You have to break out of your own routine ways of doing or accepting things. At first you may feel awkward, though once you get going it can be fun. You might have to establish the ground rules for a discussion rather than have them imposed on you. You might have to bring two dozen people to a meeting rather than the expected two. You might have a roomful of supporters all stand up and walk out of a meeting into the TV cameras. You might even have to sing a tamale song.

You will often need to dramatize the issue

Beyond engaging in new or different ways of acting, you may need to bring the spotlight to an issue. "WILL WORK FOR FOOD"—the cardboard sign was as scraggly as the man holding it. It disturbed me when I first saw this sign, this man, and a few of his brethren on the streetcorners around the city. Oh, come on, you may be thinking, do you mean you haven't seen these signs before? Now, yes, I have. Then, no. And that's the point, isn't it? These signs are so commonplace that they are rarely noticed. They cause no particular stir. The signs and the men and women holding them have faded into the landscape. We get used to things that used to disturb us, and we don't seem to notice things that affect other people more than they affect us.

Numerous items must compete for a community's attention. A few of these make it to an agenda for action. Often, items are placed on the agenda by powerful people or powerful, narrow interests. However, other items get acted on because at some point enough people in the commu-nity become alarmed, excited, or in some other way concerned about the issue. Generally, though, community awareness and concern can only fo-cus on a few matters at a time, everything else becomes so much back-ground music. As an activist, you may have to do something to thrust an issue into the limelight to provoke a response and the possibility of a new direction. This is particularly true if you are working with people who have little power.

You may need to stage some sort of a show. The show needs to have a starting and stopping point. It may be noisy or compellingly silent. It may anger people or make them laugh. It must make a point, it must get noticed, and it must lead to action. If you are successful, you will break people from their ignorance or complacency. You dramatize an issue to break through the inertia of indifference. You use it to get things going or to markedly accelerate action. Other steps must be taken to sustain action.

"Will work for food" is a statement now reduced to the butt of jokes. So how would you dramatize an issue affecting those who hold the signs?

Pick an actionable issue

Talking, grousing, accommodating—these things come easily. Changing circumstances does not. Something has to pull you to that invisible barrier that separates acceptance of dissatisfaction from action—you need a good issue.

A good issue will provoke people to action. It will give a sense of direction and provide motivation. It energizes. It brings things into focus and clarifies the things you must do. Once discovered, it won't be ignored. A good issue touches a nerve and provokes some emotion. It serves as a rallying point. If your issue is unfocused, the movement will probably flounder. If it is clear, the movement will be energized. Issues put a face on frustration. They draw the disparate colors of discontent into a clear picture that everyone can see.

A good issue makes you want to start. It helps you start. It gives you answers for the most difficult question you will face, "Where do we begin?" An actionable issue provides a picture of what is wrong or, conversely, what "better" clearly looks like:

- The clinic isn't open when people can use it.
- The girls aren't allowed to play basketball at recess.
- The police take 2 hours to respond to calls in the neighborhood.
- The caseloads are too high for anyone to do anything meaningful.
- The only history that matters happened in Europe.
- The weed strewn dirt lot invites broken wine bottles, not safe, laughing children.

With an actionable issue there is no one magic place to start, but there are usually a number of things that can be done at the beginning. You can get going, and your actions will lead you to discover other things that need to be done. You are on your way.

Create options for mutual gain

You go to the store, pick up a bag of chips, a six-pack of guava juice, a can of refried beans, some no-fat frozen yogurt, and a couple of day-old jelly donuts. An odd combination, but it works for you. You give the cashier your money and walk out of the store ready to do some serious dining. You got what you needed, and so did the store. You both gained in a transaction so simple that you take it for granted. Mutual gain—it's what makes things work.

Obviously, efforts to bring about change assert the interests of the group working for the change. That is logical. To do so exclusively—that is, only paying attention to your interests—is ineffective. Recognize the other stakeholders. What do you know about them and their interests? They certainly are going to care about those interests and try to see that they are met. You need to care about these interests too. Your ignorance or inattentiveness to others' interests may very well lead you to raise unnecessary resistance or diminish otherwise available support. It will work against you.

As you advance your own agenda, you are asking others to recognize its validity and respond appropriately. That is a legitimate request, but one that you must make of yourself as well. Your ability to recognize what is important to other stakeholders will be extremely helpful in guiding your strategy. To the extent that you can meet their interests along with yours, you will find that implementation of the change will be much easier. Agreements are made through the discovery of common ground. You may need to work creatively to find it.

You and a friend share an apartment. He is, well, not the neatest person in the world. Even though you divide up the chores, he doesn't attend to things the way you'd like. When it's his week to do dishes, they just pile up in the sink and grow over the countertops. By the end of the week he gets around to doing his chores, but you have to leave the house or turn up the TV so you don't hear the clanging of pots and the racket of his too colorful complaining. He hates it. You hate it—and you are going to change things. You decide to bring it up during your dinner of microwaved pizza and peanut butter sandwiches, but before you do, he starts in on your cooking. He thinks meals should be more elegantly crafted. When it's his week to cook you do eat pretty well. Well, of course, he loves to cook, while it's all you can do to pull something out of the freezer and stick it in the microwave. See any options for mutual gain here?

In community change situations the options may not be as clear, but there are almost always some that are present. The problem is, nobody is looking for them. Like roommates often do, various parties look at their own concerns so narrowly that they can't see anything else. It is hard to look at what is important to someone else when you are so busy feeling offended and ignored yourself.

Not all interests are obvious (stated interests are not always the real interests), and not all interests are valid. This does make things difficult. However, in most circumstances a sufficient number of valid interests can be uncovered that will lead to progress if acknowledged and acted on. You need to make it your business to find this common ground, and you also need to understand that you may have to work harder at this than other parties will. The realization that other parties won't work as hard gets in the way of some change agents. They see it as unfair, and that's enough to stop them from continuing to work. Well, it might be unfair, but is that the issue you most need to see resolved? View this as a way of getting your goals met. You are going to have to work harder at that than other parties are anyway. This is just one way that you do it. You can work hard at insisting on your interests in a totally self-serving fashion, or you can work hard at asserting your interests in recognition of the interests of others.

If you decide to undertake this approach, you will need to creatively identify and sort through the various options with the other parties. In most instances, options are discernable and the process is fairly manageable. However, in cases of significant power differentials between parties, or in cases of strong mistrust, providing benefits to other parties may be so foreign an idea that you need to struggle more to adhere to this orientation. If you act on interests the other party declares, rather than those you just assume, you will increase the meaningfulness of your actions. You will also reduce opposition by acknowledging the other party's need to have some control.

Once you set the tone for an examination of mutual gains, you will probably see that you can hold the negotiations to that standard. In most cases, stakeholders recognize the benefit of that approach, and you will see that the way everyone thinks about the situation seems to change. In almost any change episode you will have some opposition or some hesitant ally. By looking for ways both parties can gain, you will unclutter the process and save yourself a lot of headaches.

 ## Engaging Resistance and Developing Support

In most efforts to promote change, someone's routines or entrenched interests will be upset. Resistance is the companion to almost any change effort. This set of rules will help you deal more effectively with opposition. The best way to manage resistance is to build your own base of support, and a number of these rules address that issue.

Don't underestimate your opponent

"The man is an idiot." Continued inability to move an important piece of legislation out of committee had given voice to frustration. Heads nodded in agreement. The one key legislator who was blocking progress was further painted with the colors "stupid," "dense," and, from one of our more articulate artists, "obtuse."

The sad truth was that the man was not an idiot; in fact he was very clever. We hadn't counted on that, and we were probably as upset with ourselves over that miscalculation as we were angry at his performance. He didn't agree with our point of view, but he was not an idiot.

If you have an opponent who is currently resisting or attacking you, remember that you are not alone in this situation. While you are maneuvering to gain your best advantage, the other side is likely doing the same thing, or some of the same things. Frankly, though, if your group is committed to purposeful analysis and preparation for action, in most cases your opponent will not be as prepared as you are. Your dedicated sense of purpose is likely to be an advantage for you, but you cannot assume that to be the case. When you are dealing with a particularly entrenched opponent, assume that the other side is working just as hard and cleverly as you are. If it turns out that they were not working very diligently, you will be in great shape. If it turns out that they have been just as determined, you will not be caught off guard.

As you prepare to engage such an opponent, look at the situation from your opponent's point of view in terms of issues and their importance as well as strategy and tactics. With this understanding you can better anticipate your opponent's next move. You must try to counter or preempt moves as well as make the opponent respond to your moves.

Be prepared for the fact that your opponent will do something you did not anticipate. In this situation, it is usually better to stall or create a delay before acting to avoid just responding as the opponent set you up to do.

Do not assume that you are innately more capable or committed. Some who are not very effective in producing results can be quite skilled at thwarting opposition or defending themselves. So don't take your opposition for granted. Measure your response according to the importance of the threat the opposition can pose, and overestimate a bit—don't underestimate the opposition.

Give your opponents their proper due

Opponents are those individuals and groups who have some degree of commitment to preventing your success. That is, they are willing to work or otherwise act in a manner to stop you. Not every person who offers some disagreement or resistance to you will be an opponent. Some will have only a temporary interest in your matter. Some will think you are wrong, but aren't interested in fighting you. Some may simply want you to take another tack. You must be prepared to deal effectively with your real opponents, but you don't need to take on everyone.

Once you have determined that the opponent is real, act to diminish the strength of the opposition while increasing your own strength. Sometimes this involves purposeful, cooperative actions (you can turn opponents into allies), sometimes this involves direct conflict. Be careful not to focus all your energy on your opponent and lose sight of your own agenda.

In some instances overcoming an opponent may be your primary intent. That is, by changing or stopping the opponent's action, you achieve what you set out to do. Preventing a toxic waste dump from being placed in your community is an example of this. In other situations an opponent may be interfering with your ability to accomplish a particular goal—for example, by blocking your development of a new program or resisting your efforts to develop a strong parents' organization. Here, you are changing conditions or bringing something new into being. Your goal involves more than containing your adversary, although this may occupy some of your attention as you try to move forward.

The difference between these situations is that the in first case the opponent is your focus, in the second the opponent is not. By making your opponent your focus in the second case, you distract your attention from your primary purpose. You get sidetracked and halt progress toward your real goal. In short, you serve the interests of your adversary. Ideally, you should deal with your foe in a way that advances your interests. At the very least, deal with the obstacles your opponent creates while you keep advancing toward your goal—rather than in place of advancing toward your goal.

If you treat people as if they are allies, they are more likely to become allies; if you treat them as enemies, they are more likely to become enemies

She was a newly elected member of the city council: first month in office, no track record to speak of, just a bunch of campaign promises that sounded good enough to get her elected. Now here she was in City Hall, sitting with a dozen advocates representing those too long forgotten by that same City Hall, ready to listen and eager to please.

They started in on her before the sound of her welcome had died from the room. They were angry, with good cause, and they let her know it. It was a well-orchestrated meeting. Before she could finish her answer to one question, another would be fired. Everyone got in their shots. Then they left, but not before they told her that she was "like all the rest" and she'd "better look out." They had gotten to her and she felt defeated—and they knew it.

That feeling of being defeated sickened her, especially since she didn't even know she was going to be in a fight. That insulting feeling was replaced by others, among them animosity and a resolve that this would never happen to her again. She'd better look out? So should they.

Some of the work you do will rattle some cages. You are going to have enough enemies; you need not create more. Perhaps people should understand your frustration and anger over conditions. Perhaps they should know that you don't really mean to take it out on them. Perhaps they should be more sensitive and understanding. Perhaps you should know that this isn't going to happen very often.

How you treat people does not determine whether they will be allies or enemies, but it does have strong bearing on the outcome. The interests of certain people and organizations will be affected by the changes you are proposing. The desire to serve those interests will more or less naturally lead them to support or oppose you.

The mere fact that you are proposing some change may cause some who should be natural supporters to be wary. Even though the change may serve their interests, both you and the change may be somewhat un-known and unproven. Change upsets the routine and makes people ner-vous. They are not quite sure how things are going to turn out, so they may act defensively. Further, just because you know something may ben-efit another's interests doesn't mean they can readily recognize that fact. They may need some patient educating and an active invitation to assist you in meeting mutual interests before they are ready to demonstrate support.

Think about this for a moment. What does somebody want you to do that you still resist doing? Do you need to study more, stop smoking, look for a job, exercise, recycle?

Though there may be a few natural supporters and opponents, most other potential parties you encounter will be somewhat neutral. How you relate to these people could be significant in the amount of assis-tance or antagonism you will receive. Remember that it is much easier to turn an ally into an enemy than the reverse.

It does no good to inflame the animosity of those who don't intend to be helpful or who want you to fail. Neither should you fall all over yourself to be ingratiating just so some potential adversary will like you. It is better simply to keep them at arm's length or out of the picture completely.

Our fears may lead us to treat people in a way that creates a hostile response. We don't want to give them the power to reject us, and we are afraid that they will, so we strike first, more or less doing unto others be-fore they do unto use. This may not give us what we want, but it enables us to confirm our fears and put rejection more into our own hands. That we introduced the hostility is a fact we may conveniently ignore.

Although you don't want to arouse opposition due to carelessness, there may be a good reason to put someone in the role of the enemy. Per-haps they can serve as a lightning rod to draw in more support. Perhaps early on you want to put them and others on notice that your group is not to be trifled with. However, if you do make an enemy or focus on an existing one, be sure you are doing so to serve your interests, not simply because you are afraid or upset.

There are many, many potential supporters available in your arena of action. Some will be valuable even though they may offer only en-couragement. These less active friends will help cultivate the environ-ment in which change occurs. Others will become active partners, col-laborating with you to get things done. When you engage people in a way that suggests that they are friendly and helpful, they commonly re-spond that way. Your actions toward them imply that they are capable of responding well to a reasonable request. The more confident you are about yourself and the value of what you are doing, the easier it will be for you to relate to other people and organizations in a way that evokes helpful consideration.

Always ask: "Who else should we be talking to?"

If you can hold all your meetings in a phone booth, you're in big trouble. Organized change requires the interest, investment, and action of a number of individuals. Each person you approach for assistance is connected with other people who might add something to your effort. Each person. There are no exceptions. But both you and they may remain unaware of that fact unless you ask, "Who else should we be talking to?"

Organized change is a process of building. You are acquiring, assembling, and using more information, more talents, more credibility—more of everything your effort requires. By and large this all comes through people who have taken a sufficient interest in the campaign. And people most often come from connections with other people. One person can lead you to two other people, who can lead you to two others, who can lead you to still more. And the effort continues to build. Most people, especially those who see themselves as important, like to be seen as being well connected. Your "who else?" puts that belief to the test.

To take best advantage of the offer of new contact names you are given, it is helpful to ask if you can use the giver's name when making contact. Let's say you've been talking to Karen Goldman, who has given you the name of Sonny Bryans. You would simply ask, "May I tell Sonny that you suggested I contact him?" Sonny may not know you from Adam, but he does know Karen Goldman. Karen's name gives you a little better entree by making you less a stranger to Sonny. For some reason people seem reluctant to ask this question. It is a simple and important one, and since you are often speaking with people who have at least some interest in your success, you are likely to get a good response.

In addition to helping you acquire resources and connections to help you in your work, there is another important reason for asking "who else?" and following up. The question creates an awareness of your endeavor that is greater than the sum of its parts. As your existence enters the consciousness and conversations of more and more people, you begin to affect the setting in which the change is to occur. As word of your work spreads, the legitimacy and reality of what you are doing is confirmed among an expanding circle of people, many of whom may be significant players in the community affected by your intended change.

Identify stakeholders and develop investors in the change

Stakeholders are those people whose interests your actions could benefit or threaten. They are somehow involved in the situation you are addressing. What you do can arouse their reaction.

Not all these stakeholders will be evident to you from the outset. Spend some time purposefully thinking through who might be affected by what you are doing. If you fail to do this, you may have to contend with unexpected opposition, which will drain resources you intended to direct to other activities. You may also miss opportunities to strengthen or replenish the resources you need to accomplish your goals. So ask yourself:

- Who is likely to oppose us? Why?
- Who is likely to support us? Why?
- Who benefits from the current conditions? Who is harmed or irritated by them?

Do not assume that all individuals or groups who seem to have a philosophy or set of interests similar to yours will support you. Some will actually oppose you because they are getting something out of the situation you are trying to change. Don't forget that the presence of problems to some degree benefits those who see themselves as problem solvers. Problems can provide funding, prestige, and a sense of meaning to those whose business it is to deal with them. Who will like it and who won't if the problems go away?

Those who are threatened by your actions are generally more likely to react earlier and stronger than are potential supporters. This is not surprising. Opponents will need to assert themselves sooner, otherwise their task will be more difficult. Supporters don't face a similar loss. They will benefit from your actions, and you may be relieving them of some work. Additionally, they may hang back a little at first just to see if you are real.

Moving stakeholders to investors in your effort increases your resources and decreases the potential for disputes. Investors are created through contributions. The most significant contributions that lead to an investment in your success are those related to goal setting, planning, and decision making, though not all potential investors are able or interested in this sort of involvement. Anytime someone contributes to you in any way they become investors who have some heightened interest in the outcome of your efforts. Recognize this and look for ways to allow people to contribute. Then, specifically ask them. Whenever you can, nurture or strengthen the level of investment, particularly through periodic contacts that include updates on your progress. This also provides opportunities to strengthen both the level and the frequency of the contributions they are able to make.

Almost anyone is a potential investor—even some opponents. Some of those who resist you may experience a real loss if your efforts succeed, but this is not true of all who seem to get in your way. You may find it worthwhile to figure out how you can get opponents to join you or at least to end their antagonism.

Your effort will always need more investors. Unfortunately, many groups slack off as time goes on. Once they get a core group, they become complacent and don't actively seek new investors, preferring to ask for a greater investment from the few who already give a lot. This is a mistake. There will never be a time when your organization does not need new investment or increased investment from the less involved. A conscious effort to develop new owners of the effort is one of the most significant things you can do.

Put things in people's frames of reference and attention

Imagine, if you will, that you are walking through an art museum. A few people are walking about reverentially, as if they were in church. Strategically placed lights gently illuminate tastefully hung paintings. Picture yourself admiring a particularly interesting piece. Let your eyes wander over the canvas. Maybe you notice the artist's strokes or the use of color or the interplay of light and shadow. You do not notice anything outside the picture frame just now, do you? Nothing that is not captured by the frame matters much at all.

Our lives are not much different. Our lives are framed by our experiences, our skills, and the knowledge and values passed on to us that we have made our own. It is within this frame that things make sense to us. We refer to the elements within this frame to interpret new events. We draw meaning from them. They even direct our notice of the world. Anything that falls outside this frame of reference is ignored. We might not even recognize much outside that frame unless we are specifically asked or forced to. Even then, it may be hard to interpret or understand.

To attract interest in the change you are pursuing, you will need to relate your issues and actions to people's frames of reference. They will not pay attention, and they certainly will not act, if things remain outside their realm of experience, skills, knowledge, or values. You have to find a way to connect the change effort to as many of these elements as possible. The closer the fit, the better.

If you want people to move beyond general support to action, you need to call them to action when their attention is focused on the matter and they are able and in the mood to act. Let people know why they are being invited to act, and keep the invitation open while letting them know how they can act. In fact, you must repeat the invitation frequently and in different ways to catch people when they are ready to act. Invite, invite, and invite again. Otherwise, you will probably get the same, most likely shrinking, set of people over and over again.

Link those who need to know with those who do know

You don't know everything. You don't need to. As a significant person in the change effort, you may find yourself expecting to know more than you do, particularly when called on for some specific knowledge or skill. Your best answer in times like these is to provide the name of someone who can really help, and then link these people together.

In most communities, those who know useful things and those who need that very talent or information walk right by each other without ever stopping to talk. One of your important jobs is helping people find each other. When people make connections with one another, relationships begin to develop. Recalling that everything happens through relationships, you can begin to see how valuable connecting people can be. Not only do things advance as abilities are put to use but new relationships occur within the community, which increase its cohesion and strength. Even connecting people from outside the immediate community with those inside gives the community the benefit of expanding its external support. Be on the lookout for opportunities to make these connections.

Keep people involved with the effort involved with each other

It is a busy world. When one activity moves from our attention, another takes its place. Stop for a moment and reflect on some activity that you think is important. Perhaps it is a change that you are now working on. Perhaps it is something purely recreational. As you reflect, what do you see? What images come to mind?

Unless the activity is a very solitary one, it is likely that what you see when you think of something important is people. You don't see just you, and you don't see just the "work," whatever that is. You see the faces of the people who work, play, or talk with you. Community action implies relationships among people. This is self-evident. Yet the focus of our attention is often on the things we must do. Too little attention is given to relating to the people with whom we do these things.

The people in your organization *are* your organization. Not the work, not the issue itself, but the people. Their involvement and your relationship to each other is what makes things real. This shared sense of identification adds meaning to what you do. It is another element that sustains you, particularly when things are difficult. A group whose members only infrequently relate to each other around the work they must do will not be a group for very long.

The work of your organization is usually done by individuals or small groups in the days or weeks between the times that most members come together for meetings. Meetings are normally a place for discussion, decision, and acknowledgment of your efforts. Not much actual work is done there (but reaffirmation of who we are and what we do certainly is). Action-oriented groups need to see evidence of the actions its members are taking. Somehow this has to be communicated. The more uncertainty members have about each other's commitment and the more uncertainty they have about the likelihood of success, the more important this communication is. Insecurities feed on themselves, and groups lacking confidence make up things that feed their insecurities. It is not long before made-up things blur with fact. It can become almost impossible to separate the two. This is a very destructive process. If there is little contact among members, this process is likely to occur.

As a leader within your organization, your ability to fashion methods of regular contact among members will be critical to the success of your efforts. Three aspects of this contact are important. First is frequency. Although the entire organization does not need to get together all the time, various parts of the organization should keep in close touch. Second, members need to see each other and talk with each other face to face. A newsletter may keep the organization in the minds of members and keep them informed, but it does not do much toward building relationships. The more firsthand the contact the better. Finally, the contact should include time for people to work and plan together along with opportunities for people to get to know each other and to have fun together. The cohesion that comes from more solid interpersonal relationships will help hold the organization together.

Especially in a volunteer organization, and most change efforts have a strong volunteer orientation, working in isolation can be deadly. Whenever possible arrange for members to work together, particularly in pairs.

Arranging the schedules for two people is not difficult, and the benefits provided in increased accountability and partnership make this design more than worth the minimal effort it requires.

You need to communicate the progress of your work. You need to communicate its purpose. You need to communicate the presence and commitment of one another. Think of this as three sides of a triangle, each supporting the other. When you keep in contact, you can communicate these things and strengthen your connections.

Hold mutual and high expectations for people with whom you are working

Most of us can do more than we think we can, but we won't do things that we think are impossible or unreasonable. Participants in a change effort need to set high standards, encourage one another to meet them, and recognize each other for doing so. Yet these standards must be reasonable, or members will stop doing things altogether. In fact, one of the problems organizations often face is that people who have become more highly involved do not believe they can step their activity level down a notch or two, so they just drop out. Another common problem for organizations is that members expect something different from themselves than what others expect from them. Expectations are often unspoken, unclear, and unshared.

Now that you are a well-known change agent in your community, from time to time people will ask for your help. You receive a phone call. Someone asks you if you can assist with a newly developing organization. The caller promises that you don't have to meet very often, so you agree to lend a hand. Even though you were told you don't have to meet very often, they will still probably expect you once a month. Au contraire. They want you once a week—but you don't know that. The few members of this new group are excited about what they are doing, so once a week doesn't sound like much. They start calling you. You start feeling bugged. You go every other week and feel put upon. Since you miss half the meetings, they wonder if you really care at all. You get irritated with each other. You complain to members you think will agree with you. Other people complain about you. The energy and enthusiasm of the organization is drained away by this squabble, and nobody did anything bad to begin with. Each just interpreted actions as bad or wrong based on very different expectations.

What you believe some other member should be doing needs to be the same thing that they believe they should be doing. If it is not the same, count on irritation and defensiveness. Count on trouble. In my experience, more organizations are defeated by these unseen enemies within than by more powerful external opponents.

Understand that people's needs and interests change over time. Greater or lesser responsibilities may need to be worked out from time to time. Otherwise people will renegotiate their level of involvement on their own, and not tell anybody. Or worse, they will pretend they told someone or assume that the person will figure it out. Then things start to get really weird.

People don't always know just because they should. So talk to each other clearly, in a down-to-earth manner. Many problems within an organization are not the result of people doing things wrong but of doing things differently from what was expected. Having mutual and high expectations of one another promotes harmony and excellence.

Look for ways to build commitment from people

In a time when multiple distractions and transitory relationships seem to be the norm, fostering deeper commitment is indeed a challenge. You will probably benefit by first paying attention to a few general notions. To start with, understand that people join an organization for a number of reasons. They benefit from the work of the organization; they like the work the organization is doing; they like the people in the organization; or the organization benefits them in some other aspects of their lives. (More detail on group membership can be found in Napier and Gershenfeld's work; see the readings list at the end of this book.) So keep things meaningful, interesting, and enjoyable while strengthening the relationships among participants. Following the 10 steps described here will help.

1. *Help members understand the issue.* People avoid situations in which they feel ignorant. Increased knowledge will make participation more attractive. Not only will people be much more comfortable when they more fully understand what this effort is all about but they will be more dedicated as well.
2. *Help members understand the work and how to do it.* People avoid situations in which they feel incompetent. Increased ability encourages a greater interest in becoming active. Performing tasks in a competent manner is reinforcing, whereas ineptitude is frustrating. Anyone who has tried cross-stitching or golf knows this.
3. *Help members understand the organization.* People avoid situations where they don't know how to fit in. Helping participants understand

how things are organized and how their contributions make a difference can help people feel included. Further, helping people understand the nature of relationships among the participants, the special language that is likely to emerge, and some sense of the organization's history and future will lead people to feel like insiders, not outsiders.

4. *Help members get to know each other and enjoy their company.* People avoid situations in which they feel isolated. Providing opportunities for people to work together, to talk together, and to just have fun together will bring about new relationships and strengthen affiliation.

5. *Help members see progress and recognize success.* People avoid situations of stagnation or failure. Aspects of success and progress are all around you. As you and others in the organization develop a focus on gains being made, an attitude of confidence and higher expectations arises. People want to be part of a successful enterprise.

6. *Help members increase the number and complexity of tasks.* People avoid situations that have become too routine or boring. Some degree of challenge keeps interest alive. Further, this increases people's knowledge and skill while raising their awareness of the importance of their participation. Promote the notion that people can work on things that meet their personal interests and abilities. As people become more occupied with the work of the organization, they become less likely to be drawn away by other involvements.

7. *Help members increase responsibility, especially in the area of decision making.* People avoid situations over which they have little or no control or influence. Many decisions need to be made over the course of the change episode. Some will be big, some pretty small. By creating opportunities for people to have some say in the direction of the project, they have a greater ownership of the action and an increased desire for the action to be successful.

8. *Help members recognize opportunities for burden sharing.* People avoid situations in which they feel overwhelmed. A feeling that one has both permission and an opportunity to discuss a decision or to ask for help to complete an assigned task will increase members' willingness to take on more active roles. Other forms of burden sharing, such as being able to let off steam or to get help figuring out a problem, are also valuable.

9. *Help members get recognition for their contributions to the effort.* People avoid situations in which there is little recognition of their value. It is easy to publicly and privately acknowledge people and what they are doing. Recognition need not be limited to work-related

issues. People make contributions through their friendliness, sense of humor, listening abilities, and in a host of other ways. Look for things to recognize people for and confirm their value.

10. *Help people see how the work of the organization benefits them.* People avoid situations that do not relate to their interests. Linking the work and the accomplishments of the organization to what is important to people will increase the validity of their efforts.

Understanding what people avoid will help you come to see both potential barriers and opportunities for fuller participation. By purposefully creating situations that are more attractive for potential, new, and veteran members, you create conditions for increased commitment.

Periodically review this list to see how you are doing.

 ## Create and Fill Key Roles Within the Organization

This set of rules describes a number of important roles within the organization. No one person can fill all the functions an organized effort requires. By identifying a range of contributing roles, you help build investment and leadership.

Formalize the role of the Nag

You can almost see the energy draining from the room, seeping out of the smiles and rolling right out the little space between the floor and the tightly shut door. It just disappears. Everything seems to sag just a bit now that the third person in a row has sheepishly confided that he too hasn't been able to get something done that he promised to do. The required nodding of indulgent heads and the tolerant mumblings of "that's okay" accompany a background chorus of creaks as people begin to shift a little uncomfortably in their seats. Things aren't going anywhere and everybody knows it.

Most of us do intend to do the things we commit to at a meeting, but the distractions of the everyday world often leave our well-intentioned promises locked in the "I'll get to it when I can" closet. Sometimes we forget to open that closet door. Then we realize too late that we didn't take care of something we said we were going to do. It's embarrassing. It's not long before people stop showing up for meetings if they have nothing but excuses to talk about. Not much longer after that no one shows up, or two or three people end up doing everything.

How can action groups deal with this very normal dilemma? Appoint a Nag. Or, if the members of the group haven't developed a sense of humor yet, you can call this person the "follow-up coordinator."

The Nag is an extremely valuable person, one that every group should have. The key here is that this role must be understood, formalized, and mutually accepted. The group needs to clarify what this person's job is and agree to select a particular person to do it. This is definitely not a role someone just decides by themselves to start doing. If so, other people will feel, well, nagged. Creating the role of the Nag must be a group decision.

Basically, the Nag does three things:

- Records everyone's commitments during the meeting.
- At the end of the meeting, reads back the commitments (along with completion dates) to make sure everyone has the same understanding.
- A few days before a task is to be completed, the Nag calls the person responsible for the task "to see how things are going."

Although the Nag may help the other person figure out how to complete the task, the Nag does not assume any responsibility for doing the work. This is really a very friendly reminder call. It brings people's commitments back to their attention so they can act on them.

When the role is agreed upon and understood, the Nag's call helps to reinforce the idea that the organization is working, that people (in this case the Nag) are doing what they are supposed to be doing. The recognition that others are fulfilling their responsibilities encourages a much higher degree of follow-through.

This job is so important that the Nag should rarely take on any other responsibilities for the group.

Fill the role of the facilitator

Most groups who come together to promote change have a few individuals who are more confident in offering their ideas than others. They may be quicker to understand things or to figure out some of the things that need to be done. They may readily voice opinions about what's wrong. They often do most of the directing. They certainly do most of the talking. They are seen as the leaders. When the group meets, they run the show. The problem is, they may not be good at running the show.

When people gather together to discuss problems and potential solutions, they all come as potential contributors. The most effective organizations build a strong sense of affiliation among members and effectively utilize what each is able to offer. This is comes into focus particularly during meetings. The ability to draw out interest, ideas, and commitment so that clear decisions can be made and acted on is a particular leadership skill. It is quite apart from voicing opinions or telling people what to do.

Choose someone to fill the role of facilitator. This is a person who everyone agrees should guide the discussion. The person selected should take this responsibility seriously. This is an important step. Otherwise, the conversation may roam aimlessly. Most of us don't like to be seen as pushy or rude or know-it-alls, so often no one steps forward to guide the discussion. At the other extreme is the person who tries to run the discussion to meet his or her own interests. When this occurs, some participants will hesitate to offer their thoughts and opinions, and others may engage in a subtle (or not so subtle) power struggle with the more dominant individual. As a result, issues of power and control or fear of rejection assume greater importance than the community issues the group thinks it is talking about. Make no mistake, matters of power and control are always present to some degree. A facilitator who is clearly recognized will decrease the influence these matters will have on the discussion.

So, what should the facilitator do? To "facilitate" means to "make easy." The facilitator job is to make it easy for all members to understand and participate in the discussion, while keeping it on track. The facilitator will offer more direction and less of his or her own ideas on the matter being discussed. Key actions the facilitator will take include:

- Keeping the group on track by gently reminding them of the subject at hand and bringing the discussion back to the topic
- Guiding the group through the steps of any planned group activities
- Keeping an eye on the time
- Periodically summarizing the main points that are being made
- Recognizing signs of emerging agreement and calling these to the group's attention
- Playing "traffic cop" by recognizing those whose "turn" it is to speak and giving them the green light to do so
- Drawing out quiet members by specifically inviting their thoughts and waiting patiently for a reply
- Monitoring the emotional climate of the group and acknowledging when a particular topic is difficult to discuss or when another topic creates excitement
- Noting when a topic seems to have been adequately discussed and moving to a decision or a new topic

If the facilitator attends to these basic actions, the conversation will be productive.

In most cases the facilitator will not have been trained to perform this role. You may need to talk for a few minutes about your expectations for how the conversation should be guided and the importance of being patient with one another, remembering that many of us are just learning how to do all this.

Make use of a Notifier

Regular monthly meeting, everybody knows about it—not even half the people show up. This can feel a little discouraging. Call people a day or two before the meeting and your attendance will increase.

We shouldn't have to do that, you might be thinking. People have calendars, and they can look for themselves. Yes, they can. But some won't, and others will just ignore it

You cannot assume that if people care they will show up to a planned activity—or the reverse, that if they don't show up they don't care. People do forget, and people do have competing priorities. A phone call from a member of the group may be just enough to elevate this priority above some other ones. It reminds people of their commitment. It places the activity in their immediate frame of reference so they can act on it. It reinforces the idea that their participation matters and is counted on. There is something very powerful about a personal contact. I guarantee that this will increase participation.

The Notifier's main job is simply to call everyone, usually two days before some scheduled activity that requires their involvement. The Notifier can also be used to alert members to an upcoming event or special activity that they may not know about. An alternative to the Notifier is using a simple notification system, such as having Joe call Raul, who calls Deborah, who calls the next person in line, and so on. This can work for groups fewer than 10. (In such a system the circle of calls must be completed within a designated time period. If the initiator does not receive a call within that time to indicate that the circle is complete, he or she will initiate calls in the opposite direction. The person receiving two calls then calls the initiator to confirm that the circle has been completed.)

The Notifier role is appropriate for groups of fewer than 20 members. An organization that wants to mobilize a large number of people in a short period of time will need to develop some sort of structured alert network. This may involve a telephone tree, telephone bank, or an E-mail distribution list.

Similar to the role of the Nag, the Notifier should be an agreed-upon role and should be selected by the group. I will warn you that as soon as you suggest this idea you may very well be met with some verse of the "we don't need that, we're all adults" song. Well, maybe we're all just old children. The "we're all adults" line may really imply "don't remind me of my responsibilities." Most adults have just short of a million things on their minds. A little reminder can come in handy.

Having a Notifier or some other simple notification system will noticeably increase your participation, and the more that people get used to participating, the more they will feel identified with the effort.

Find a spark plug

Confusion over just what you are supposed to be doing, the loss of a few early members, longer than necessary meetings—these are a few of the things that can wear on your enthusiasm. All are common occurrences in any change effort, and they are noticed more if no one is around who picks things up.

You're going to need a spark plug—a person who fairly hums with energy, who can put a charge into everyone around. A spark plug will get things going and, with bursts of enthusiasm, help keep things going. The spark plug brings a zest into what he or she does, with an expectation that other people will be pretty enthusiastic too. This is a very valuable person.

Your change effort needs more than good information, clear plans, and concerned people. It needs some life. Work can become tedious, and a few letdowns are inevitable. Without someone who provides some vitality, things can grind to a dull standstill.

The best spark plugs are more than cheerleaders. They are oriented toward getting things done while keeping things upbeat. They keep the group in focus and notice progress. A good spark plug will avoid the risk of getting so caught up in things that she or he ends up doing most of the work. (Spark plugs can get burned out too.) Their enthusiasm is real and goal-directed. Their spirit is contagious, and other people will become more energetic and encouraging to one another.

You know somebody like this. Who is it?

 ## Strengthening Your Organization

The way in which you take action to promote change can attract people to your organization and strengthen the way it operates. Of course, the opposite may be true as well. This set of rules offers some guidance for developing your organization while you are putting it to use.

Tasks need to be clear, manageable, and related

Most people who begin participating really do want to help, but they may not know how. Those of you who are more active need to consciously help other participants become involved in meaningful activities that benefit the organization. It is not uncommon that people who want to contribute are responding to some vague expectation to help out, with anything. No one, though, really has a clear idea of what "anything" actually means. It is often difficult to find some worthwhile entry point, some way to get started and to make a real contribution.

If those who are more responsible for directing the work of the organization would stop for a moment to recognize this issue and deal with it directly, more work would be done by more people. A further result would be an increase in morale and a decrease in the loss of membership. This is hard to do when you are in the middle of things, yet it is necessary. No one can get to the middle of things when he or she is stuck out there at the edge of the effort.

Tasks should, first of all, be *clear*. People need to know what they are supposed to do and how it is to be done. They need to know whether or not there is an expected way for the task to be completed. In either case, some guidance would help.

You have a clear perception of a task if you can describe what it looks like when it is done. If you don't have such a clear picture in your own mind, it will be next to impossible to communicate it. A lack of clarity can lead to anxiety and frustration on everyone's part, and work that is done incompletely or incorrectly saps everyone's enthusiasm. The reverse is also true. When tasks are clear, the person charged with the work can more easily and truly accept responsibility in the first place and feel a sense of accomplishment when the task is clearly completed. Success encourages more active participation.

Tasks need to be *manageable*. Tasks should fit within the available time and talent of the people performing them. People's time and talents can grow along with their interest and experience. Individuals who do not yet have a strong investment in the effort can probably do more than they say they can or even think they can. This isn't something you can tell someone though, let them discover it on their own. After a while some will offer to take on a little more responsibility. Others may need an invitation to do a little more or to do something different, and if they are ready, they will respond.

Conversely, individuals who have a strong commitment probably can do a little less than they say or think they can. Their interest in making sure that things get done may lead them to accept more responsibility than they can actually handle well. This is particularly true for individuals who are involved with other projects along with this one. So willing are they to take on more work that you may need to first specifically ask other people to take on a particular job.

Tasks need to be *related*. We like to have a sense that what we do matters. We are more enthusiastic when we can see how our work contributes. An assignment can't just be out there by itself, just a job, apart from anything meaningful. Actions are perceived as meaningful when they are seen as connected to some end we desire or connected to other actions that are intended to produce some desired end result.

A program to produce change is similar to most other enterprises. One piece of work fits into another piece, and together all the pieces make up the whole. The more clearly participants can see the relationship between what they are doing and what "we are trying to do," the more they are able to commit to the task at hand.

Remember also that certain parts of the work need to be the responsibility of a certain person or set of persons. Things that are everyone's responsibility often become no one's.

Tasks that are clear, manageable, and related are done well. The extra minute or two you spend to see that these criteria are met will produce more results than anything else you could be doing with that time.

Use time wisely; it is a resource in limited supply

How you budget your money and how you budget your time are clear indicators of what you believe to be important. We seem to be more conscious of our money. We spend it to get by or to buy a temporary smile. We occasionally invest it to get more. We horde it against the day our best efforts don't meet up with the demand at the door. We may even define ourselves by its absence or presence in our lives.

Time. We get a new supply, the same amount, each day. Maybe we know what time it is, but we may not be so clear about where time has gone. We may try to protect it, to save it, or even to change it. But at the end of the day, time is gone, and we can't bring it back. Time is something we cannot not use. The real question is how to use it.

It may be hard to see time as a resource because it's just there. We don't have to do anything to get it, and everybody has the same amount each day. We may not attend to it quite the way we do our money, yet many people in America speak of it as if it were the same. They "spend" it.

You spend it. You spend it complaining about how bad things are. You spend it talking about who should be doing what to make things better. You spend it waiting around. You spend it figuring out what you can do. You spend it in meetings. You spend it in writing. You spend it on the phone. You spend it in quiet conversation with friends.

You invest your time involving other people so that their time enriches the effort. You realize that eight people together for an hour spend eight person hours, as much time together in that one hour as a person uses in an entire workday. So you invest your time organizing work to best utilize all that time and all those talents. You invest time in one another, recognizing the value and simple joy of each other's company. You invest time playing, knowing it refreshes you and knowing that enjoying life is priceless itself. You invest your time in quiet reflection, learning.

Change does not take time. It takes thought and action. But change results from the use of time. As you proceed with your change effort, time will be one of your most fundamental and valuable resources. How will you spend it?

Your change effort better travel with a spare tire

Every change effort will encounter hazardous road conditions on the journey to success. It never fails—something will fail. It will rain when it is supposed to be sunny. Your guest speaker will come down with the flu. Your big meeting will be attended by three people, one of them being the reporter from the newspaper. For every event, something can go wrong, so you had better be prepared.

You will be able to prevent a possible catastrophe or two by anticipating what might go wrong to alert you to some steps you can take in advance. Still, things will go awry. In actual practice few of these will be catastrophes, even though at the moment of their unfolding they sure look and feel like it.

The more you are prepared with a set of backup actions, the more confidently you will handle the occasional pothole. You cannot and should not spend all your time worrying. In fact, that is why you prepare. Give attention to your backup preparations according to the degree that the event or activity is complex or important. It's not your best tire; it's just a spare tire to get you through. Basically, you want to know what to do when you can't do what you want to do.

Stand back every now and then to look at things

It is easy to get caught up in all the things you need to do. Sometimes you might feel as if you have a phone surgically attached to one ear, a keyboard superglued to your fingertips, and a "to do" list imbedded in your retina. No matter where you look, you see undone tasks. This can be as intoxicating as it is tiring.

Even when things slow down to a moderate frenzy, you can get so focused on all the little things in front of you that you lose sight of the broader picture. You might find yourself going from problem to problem or decision to decision as if only the information from the situation at hand matters. In trying to figure out how to meet your immediate challenges, you may forget some important lessons you have already learned that can help you.

Take time to collect not only your thoughts but your learning from other experiences to see what insights can guide your actions. Your immediate experience is not unconnected from your other experiences.

Hang up the phone, turn off the computer, close your eyes, or gaze at the ceiling. Take time to reflect. It is important to stand back from your immediate situation, looking at it through the lens of your experience and ask, "What principles apply here?" You may even grab a pen and jot down a few ideas to remember. Ask yourself not only "What do I know about this situation?" but "What do I know?"

Don't start with the most important thing; start with the most interesting thing

It's an hour into the meeting, and the scraping of the metal folding chairs on the church basement floor lets you know that people are getting restless. You have been talking tonight about "the things we need to do something about." Maybe you have been talking about this for weeks, maybe even years. You even have a list of all these things. You have decided to select something to *work* on. Finally.

Stop—before you do something important! If you aren't careful, people will decide which is the most important matter they face and put that at the top of the "to do" list. This might be informative, but it may very well *not* lead to sustained action. You don't need important; you need interesting or maybe exciting or perhaps even kind of easy. You can build to important once you have the power and confidence that comes with accomplishment.

Select something people can actually see themselves working on—something they want to do, not something they think they should do. What matters more is that people think they can succeed, that they could even have fun, that they will feel good and confident about what they are doing.

So before you begin whatever fancy voting process you are going to use, do let people know what it is they are voting on. They are selecting something they really want to do, something they are personally willing to work on. It doesn't even have to be important.

Meetings that produce nothing but future meetings are the death of the movement

You are having another meeting. It's on everyone's calendar, arranged after date-selecting negotiations that would make arms reductions talks look simple. You met Thursday, two weeks ago. And you met a week or so before that. You are meeting now. Nothing happens. So you decide to have another meeting.

Meetings face two very common problems. First, we are commonly not clear about just why we are meeting. What is the meeting supposed to produce? Second, most people who run meetings don't know how to do it. Meetings that don't have either of these problems are uncommon. (See the O. M. Collective's manual in the readings list for more on this.)

There are many reasons to have a meeting. Information sharing, planning, and strengthening the feeling of group membership are a few. For action-oriented groups there is an added requirement: Each meeting must, at the very minimum, produce decisions. Action-oriented groups must keep moving. They need to keep doing things. As a result, each meeting should produce clear decisions on:

- *specific* tasks to be performed by
- *specific* people according to a
- *specific* date.

Specific, remember that word. Notice how often people will back off a bit when they come close to clear decisions and assignments. You will be tempted to do the same thing. By keeping things vague, we can achieve the feeling of progress without anyone having to commit to doing anything. Whenever you allow for vagueness in any of these three critical areas, you are agreeing to slow your progress because you are keeping open questions that must be answered before action can be taken.

You run several risks if clear decisions are not made. You run the risk that vagueness will lead to inaction because people don't quite know what is expected. A lack of clarity also fosters internal dissensions by inviting different interpretations on what the actual decisions have been. A different risk you may face is that those among you who really want things to get done will just go ahead and do things themselves. Over time, a rather short time, they will expect and be expected to do most of the clarifying and most of the work, usually apart from all but a few other members of the group. They will stop asking, and the group will stop making clear decisions. A few people will run things, leading to all the problems—dwindling group interest, neglected leadership development, resentment, and burnout—that such a configuration produces. If any of these conditions apply, your meetings will not produce decisions. They will produce either hesitation or confirmation of the decisions of a few.

You will notice that the less your group makes action-oriented decisions, the less likely it will want to. You will probably have to set another meeting to discuss that.

Work to develop capability, not just to solve problems

Organizing people to promote change can involve more than just fixing a specific problem. Productive organizing includes the intent to increase the capability of people to respond meaningfully and effectively in the face of future challenges.

A number of skills are common to most change efforts, talents like providing leadership, recruiting other participants, raising and managing money, doing issue research, planning, conducting meetings, public speaking, functioning as a productive team, and developing strategies and tactics to name but a few. Added to these are skills that might be required by the specific circumstance, such as conflict resolution, lobbying, or working with the media.

A more experienced change agent will be aware of the various abilities that are needed in the situation he or she is facing, but even those with little experience will have some fairly good impressions of what these might be. This awareness creates opportunities. It challenges the change agent to be alert to skills currently available among the members of the community seeking the change and which need to be directly taught.

Though few individuals will be specifically trained in community change, many skills learned elsewhere transfer to this arena. Matching present skills to organizational needs gives members and potential members an avenue for meaningful involvement, and it reminds the community that it already has some degree of capability. Still, from those who have a head start to those who know relatively little, almost everyone will need to learn more. Few people have practiced the particular skills that working for change requires.

My friend Lou coaches a T-ball team of little kids just learning the game of baseball. The ball is set on a batting tee about waist high, making it pretty easy to hit. The young sluggers stand next to the tee and give a mighty rip, or something that approximates a mighty rip. Once the ball goes bounding toward the variously arranged fielders, a semblance of baseball begins to occur. If not otherwise engaged in watching ants making their journey through some part of the infield or talking to their newly met best friends, fielders field, runners run, and the crowd cheers.

By the end of the game almost everyone learns a little bit more about the grand old game. By the end of the season they certainly do. That is, if everyone plays. On Lou's team they do. They all have a turn in the batting order, and they all have a place in the field. Sure, Lou likes to win, but he also understands that an important part of the process is to have kids like the game and become more confident playing it. If only the skilled players play, the others will never get a chance to learn. They certainly won't develop much confidence, and they probably won't care much about the game for long.

Success may be much more important in a change effort, and most participants are adults (or at least older) and not little kids, but there are some lessons to be learned from the way Lou coaches his team. Many of us have rudimentary skills and uncertain confidence in playing this game. If most members are relegated to the bench, we probably won't get better—and we might walk away from the game altogether. True, you do not want your chances for success riding only on the bench players, but you can have a proper mix of more and less skilled members working together. As with most learning, there will be some mistakes along the way. You all will need both practice and patience.

Understand that the organization's need for a skill provides members with the chance to learn it. Purposely make opportunities available for participants to learn new skills and practice them. Pay attention both to the immediate goal the group is trying to achieve as well as to the process of increasing overall group capability. The more that required skills can be provided by members of the community who desire the change, the more capable that community will be. It will be able to fix many more problems than the one it may now be facing.

Play to your strengths

Your community has strengths. Your organization has strengths. You have personal strengths. Let these define who you are and how you will proceed.

Starting with yourself, do you know what you are good at? What do you have, or what can you do that might be useful to the change effort? What is it that you can turn to when things get difficult?

If you are not aware of these assets, or you don't value them, how can you really use them? Recognize and value your strengths, and as you use them they will develop even more. Their presence in your awareness emboldens you.

I began cleaning up the shed the other day and was amazed at what I found. Three caulking guns. I didn't know I had any. Apparently, I didn't know that on several occasions. A glue gun, and a staple gun also got added to my arsenal somewhere along the way. It was beginning to look like I had planned to do battle with all sorts of enemies of household upkeep. I also discovered a whole package of new washers for spigots, hose attachments, and other contraptions given to dripping. There was more. A pop rivet set, two old fishing reels, and three C-clamps of various sizes. As my cleaning frenzy accelerated, even more treasures were uncovered. I started envisioning how I might use this stuff, and I got to feeling a little giddy at the prospects. I also remembered projects unattempted or undone because I didn't have what I needed. Well, I did have what I needed. I just forgot to really check.

When you think of your organization what comes to mind? Do you recognize that your organization is rich in abilities? Sure, some members will squabble, some won't follow through on commitments, and a few will act a little quirky now and then. These things happen in your organization, but they aren't your organization. What is it that your organization has going for it? What sources of strength can it draw from, if only it would notice? This is the perception of your organization that will motivate you and help you plan strategies. Your community is much the same. It too has much to offer.

Just what are strengths? They are skills, like artistic talent or computer wizardry. They are intangible capital, like energy and enthusiasm. They are qualities, like patience and understanding. They are advantages, like public attention or sympathy. They are aptitudes for learning. They are connections with important people or many people. They are friendships and more. In short, strengths are anything that can help you meet your challenges.

When you come up against what you need to do, especially what you feel unable to do, play to your strengths. If your organization were to develop a plan of action based on what you could do or could easily learn to do, would that look different from what you are doing today? If you met challenges based on what strengths you have available to you rather than what you fear, would that look any different?

Pay regular attention to what you have going for you. Turn the challenges you face to meet your strengths. Use your strengths to determine which projects to undertake and how to tackle them. Go look in your shed.

Keep your edge

When people are geared up to do something, try to prevent any delay from occurring. Canceled activities or events that have to be rescheduled can dull things. If you are going to generate interest, take pains to make sure that you are going to be able to put it to use.

Sometimes things build energy on their own, and people really want to take action, whether you primed this atmosphere or not. If this is the case, find some way that a constructive action can be taken.

Periodic activity helps maintain a state of readiness. It becomes difficult to rekindle interest once you have let it cool.

Understand the action–involvement–communication–decision cycle of empowerment

Everything starts with *action*. It is both the final step and the first one. If you do not take frequent, sufficient, and meaningful action, your organization will stagnate. Planning is not action, nor is talking about the problems you face. Action involves both individual and group performance of tasks or participation in events that are directly related to changing current conditions. Action is your reason for being. It provides focus and meaning. It confirms your purpose.

Action leads to the *involvement* of other people. It will automatically attract attention and interest in your cause. On its own, action can also attract people to your organization. This natural tendency can be intensified by consciously using action or activities that lead to action to draw more people into the effort. Ask yourself, "How can we use this activity to get more people to join us?" Inviting people to take part in a specific activity gives them a concrete way to be involved.

As long as your organization exists you will need to involve more people. There will always be some loss of membership. Some people will become less interested, others may leave the community, still others will have personal matters that demand more of their attention. You will need to do more than replace these lost members. You will need to continually increase your numbers. Increased numbers give you credibility, confidence, and access to more people with talents and connections. People are resources, and you will never have too many resources.

Routine and frequent *communication* is necessary to maintain involvement and promote task accomplishment. You must keep in communication. Today, with our many diverse commitments pulling us in different directions, it is easy to become distracted and move our attention off the activities of the organization and the people involved in it. Members of action groups need to keep in communication to keep up with the project and to stay in touch with each other.

Communication counters feelings of isolation and worry over progress. When communication declines, so does participation. Uncertainty is the frequent guest to something new. People are not sure if their concerns are widely shared, and they often question the likelihood of success. Breaks in communication foster that uncertainty. In the face of the unknown, people will frequently make up things to feed their insecurities. Members need communication for the change effort to remain real and important in their minds.

Misunderstandings, energy wasted when changes in directions are not communicated, and other difficulties occur when communication drops off. Frequent and effective communication can prevent these and other difficulties that erode confidence and motivation. Communication keeps the organization in tune. At a practical level, communication helps get the work done. Assignments are made and monitored. Directions are provided. Help and encouragement are given where needed. The relationship of specific responsibilities to the overall effort is made clear. Completion of one set of tasks moves a new set of tasks into view. These receive their due attention and, in turn, give way to succeeding tasks. Progress is noted.

Communication leads to a greater awareness of what needs to be done. It helps the group to know who can help and what challenges and opportunities lie ahead. This understanding demands decisions.

"We've been working on this for the last three years." Groups that are stuck seem to say things like that. You have probably heard similar statements a time or two. In my experience these groups haven't been doing much work in the last three years. In fact, if you were to count all the actual work that had been done, it might add up to, oh, two or three weeks during that time. A more accurate statement might be, "We've been worrying about this for the last three years" or "We have been talking about this for the last three years." All of this takes a toll, and it *feels* like work. Holding on to some discomfort without making an active decision to get rid of it can be very tiring indeed.

Decisions must be made for action to occur—clear decisions. Remember, each meeting needs to produce decisions about *specific* acts, which will be done by *specific* people, according to a *specific* date. These decisions imply an even more powerful decision—the decision to be successful.

Decisions are given life through action. Taking action leads to more involvement, more communication, more decisions, more action, and more involvement. This cycle creates a powerful community. Each of these elements is essential; none can be ignored or taken for granted. If you remove any one of these elements, things will grind to a halt.

CHAPTER 6

Things to Know About People

People are more similar than they are different. We all have similar needs. We all have similar responses to problem situations. We all have similar fundamental hopes. How we express these things may vary among cultures and among people within the same culture. These differences are real and valid. Still, trying to understand one another according to our differences is futile and misleading. It is our similarities that bind us.

Nothing is more valuable to any change effort than the people involved in it. People are what put any other resource into action. When you organize a community, you organize people. So, what do you know about this most critical element of your change effort?

Why people do what they do is one of life's enduring mysteries. The rules described in this chapter address some of the more important observations about people, particularly when they are engaged in a change effort. Some of these people will be participants seeking the change. Others may be the targets of strategies and tactics employed by those promoting the change. When you read over this list, see which ones particularly apply to you.

Most of the people who will work with you will be volunteering their efforts as together you try to make a difference. This adds a special quality to their relationship to the work and to one another. Volunteers do not pay to participate, and they are not paid for their participation—not in money anyway. Volunteers choose the nature, degree, and frequency of their involvement. This is very different from other kinds of affiliations. A change agent must be careful to strengthen participants' ties to the meaning of the work and the importance of relationships.

Not everyone will act just the way these rules imply. Indeed, we may not always act these ways ourselves. Nonetheless, the actions and reactions set forth in these rules are common enough that you will do well to pay close attention to them.

You will see that some of the themes from earlier chapters relate to the things you need to know as you work with or in opposition to people. As you read through the rules in this chapter, you will see how each touches on some aspect of these themes. People's desire to be helpful and the importance of people receiving acceptance and gaining confidence are rooted in these elements, as are the factors that lead to action or inaction. Now let's examine these underlying themes.

When working with people involved in a change effort, start with the belief that each person has value.   Each person has something to contribute. With this starting point, you can more easily handle the inevitable human foibles you will come to recognize. With your belief in the value of each participant, you will more actively provide opportunities that will make it easy and likely for people to use the talents they have. Operating out of basic respect is empowering for all parties.

When working with people involved in a change effort, realize that some degree of uncertainty and insecurity are common.   The process of change necessarily involves rejecting the routine in favor of the new, the different, or the unknown. Change usually invites risk and some reliance on untested abilities. As a change agent, you will take steps to promote confidence. Understand that during times of insecurity people may be less tolerant of one another, so it is important to encourage participants to be patient and accepting of one another.

Most of the people who will work for the change are to some extent uncertain about what they should do and how they fit into the scheme of things. They may be unsure about the prospects for success as well. Most participants are not the early leaders. It is not surprising for levels of individual confidence to be somewhat low, even among people who are confident in other aspects of their lives. You will need to pay particular attention to this aspect of community change work.

When working with people involved in a change effort, recognize that they have a basic intent to do good and to perform well.   Understand also that the intent to do good may have to work its way through some prevailing notions that people are supposed to be self-serving. It is not naive to be altruistic. Not only is altruism in our self-interest, it is satisfying.

When working with people involved in a change effort, continue to cultivate interest and sustain involvement. There is no doubt about it, the work of change is work. It is easy for people to feel overwhelmed or directionless. Work can be managed to allow people to perform at their level of ability and interest while increasing that ability and interest. Participants' efforts need to be recognized. The activities of the organization must include more than just work. Activities that strengthen relationships and group identity are very valuable. So is taking time just to have fun.

When working with people involved in a change effort, realize that emotion is the basic contributor to action and reaction. This is true for both those who participate with you and for those who oppose you. The way people feel about something or the feelings certain issues or events provoke are at the root of how and to what extent people will respond. As a change agent, you may need to provoke, irritate, encourage, or inspire. You need to get people to feel.

When working with people involved in a change effort, expect that mistakes will be made and that they are part of the process of growth. Of course, growth comes from learning from our mistakes, not just from making them. As a change agent, you will make your share of mistakes. Your ability to accept them and to act on the discoveries they offer will help set the tone for the organization.

When working with people involved in a change effort, accept the fact that contradictory inclinations will be operating. For example, people might want to be left alone and, at the same time, want to be included. Some of this will make sense, some of it will not. Often it is just a question of balancing competing internal interests. By accepting this fact you can help people within the group find their appropriate balance. Or you may just need to understand that they are trying to work it out.

When working with people involved in a change effort, appreciate the fact that their participation is affected by their work on their relationships as well as their work on the issue. The matter of the organization is fundamentally linked to matters of people relating to one another. People will be concerned with who they are or are perceived to be in relationship to others. Their enthusiasm for the work will be affected by the quality of their relationships. Most of these matters are so routine as to be almost invisible. As a change agent, your awareness that people need to attend to their relationships as well as their work will help explain things that you see. It will also give you some ideas about how that work can be done.

When working with people involved in a change effort, don't be surprised when people act normally.   True, when united in a noble cause, people tend to act in a noble fashion. But they generally don't act perfectly. All behavior is intended to meet some need. Your opponents will act to meet their needs, as will your partners. The way you structure the operation of your organization and the tactics you employ will help you get the responses you need for your group to achieve its goals.

The life and effectiveness of your organization will be affected by your responses to these theme elements. Organizations will act pretty much as people do. Not a surprising fact since organizations are simply collections of people.

Community action implies relationships among people. This is self-evident. Yet when the topic of community work is written about, a great deal of attention is devoted to the things we must do. Perhaps too little attention is given to relating to the people with whom we do these things. When you come down to it, most of the Rules of the Game involve ways to increase your effectiveness in dealing with people. As you go about the work of change, observe how people react in various circumstances. Ask yourself what these reactions might indicate that would be important for you to remember. Then add to this list a few rules of your own.

 ## Most People Have a Desire to Be Helpful

Recognizing the fact that people involved in a change effort do want to contribute, not avoid work, will affect the way you relate to them. This set of rules provides you with a useful perspective for understanding people's intentions to be helpful, and some of the things that might get in the way.

People are basically good and want to do good things; if given half a chance, they will

Exceptions to this rule get far more attention than they deserve. Our fear about the exceptions and our tendency to succumb to discouraging pictures shown on the six o'clock news undermines our ability to believe in what is commonly much more present around us. It keeps us apart from one another and coaxes us to keep our inclinations toward altruism hidden from ourselves and others. To act on our belief in our humane nature and to be moved toward goodness appear foolish.

How foolish? The things we make up out of our insecurities and disconnectedness certainly do get in our way. Our insecurities will have us believe that most others will do us harm if we let them. A few will do harm, and we cannot be blind to that possibility nor unprepared for it. A greater number will do us good if we let them. We cannot be blind to that possibility nor unprepared for it either.

Our disconnectedness does increase the chance of exploitation and offense. Our lack of ability to recognize that we are in relationship to one another decreases the value of that relationship and the value of unknown individual others. The pursuit of self-interest in disregard of that relationship becomes more likely, confirming our fears. Left uninterrupted, fragmentation could lead to even more blind pursuit of self-interest, in turn exacerbating the cycle of disintegration and making each person more likely to be preyed upon.

Altruism is in our self-interest. At some fundamental level I believe that we know that altruism is a form of self-interest. Our ability to offer dignity raises the possibility that we will be recipients of it as well. The inclination toward humanitarian action exists within most people and is fairly strong when unlocked However, the more that individuals or groups are fearful and disconnected from the community, the more difficult it is for them to unlock.

In my experience with diverse groups of people organizing to promote change or in some way strengthen a community, I have watched people become a little or a lot amazed at the recognition of their shared belief in justice and in basic caring for other people. This is a recognition I nudge along. Sometimes disclosure of these basic beliefs has to make its way through cynicism and other forms of mistrust. A kind of embarrassment and vulnerability in acknowledging this morality often exists. Good people seem afraid that others might think them naive, a terrible sin in an era of sophistication.

It has now become fairly common for me to hear a group effectively working for change make reference to how special they are. What good people they seem to be lucky to have involved in their group. The thing that is most special about these groups is that they have simply given themselves permission to act on their better natures, to do what they wanted to do in the first place. This is liberating. The nitty-gritty business of strategies and tactics, of organizing to build power and to do the work that needs to get done, is made much easier when people have dropped the façade of cynicism.

People are willing to provide help, given the right circumstances

Assume that people will help you. This orientation is much more productive than hoping that they will help you, or expecting that they probably won't. Making the assumption that people will help you will affect the way you treat them. You will approach them with matter of fact confidence as potential partners or investors, rather than wheedling or acting apologetically. Dealing with people as if they don't want to help invents reluctance that may not be there at all.

What might be the right circumstances? First, it helps to create the circumstance by asking. I'm not kidding. Sometimes those who work for change just assume that people should or will help out because the issue is so self-evidently right and good. A few will, but most need to be asked. The more direct the request, the better. Face to face is best. Capitalize on any attention you receive, and particularly seek assistance during any periods of community enthusiasm.

It is better to ask for help when you actually need the help rather than asking for help for some future possibility. Also, people are more responsive if they are not currently engaged in some other activity when asked. Your prospects further increase if people have an interest in the matter. A final tip: When you can show that what you are asking for is easy to do, specific, and time limited, you can usually expect a favorable answer.

People are willing to do things, but they just can't seem to start

The hardest thing to do is to start. You must overcome the powerful inertia rooted in the known and the way things are. Imagine yourself trying to push a stalled car. It only weighs 3,000 pounds or so. Maybe with a lot of grunting and sweating and some help from a friend or two you finally get the thing moving. If you are on level ground, it is pretty easy to keep it rolling. It's getting it moving in the first place that is the most difficult.

Most of us are like that car. We may want something to be different or we may be agreeable to taking on a few jobs, but it is hard to get started. It is difficult to move from what we're doing now to doing something very different. This may be compounded by the fact that we are not familiar with those different activities.

Understand that this inertia creates a kind of resistance even among those people who are truly willing to help out. Don't' give up on people too early. Give them an easy place to start. Maybe even give them a friend or two to help get things rolling.

Each person has something to contribute

A month ago we divided a small neighborhood into sections, and each person had agreed to take a section, going door-to-door talking with residents about their irritations and hopes. We planned to have the whole neighborhood covered within a month. Once a week we met to review our progress and our learning. A few people had gotten a great start that first week, and everyone had made at least a few contacts—except Connie.

During the second week, even more work was done. People seemed to be getting into the excitement of an organized effort—except Connie. She had a lot of things come up at work, and she hadn't been able to do anything—but she would next week.

At next week's get-together, almost half of the group had completed their work, and everyone else was getting close. Momentum and enthusiasm were building—except for Connie. She hadn't been feeling well last week, and, no, she didn't need any help. She would really work hard next week.

Last meeting of the month. Everyone was done, almost. Everyone was trying not to look at Connie. "I'm just afraid to meet people. I can't do that," she said in announcing that once again she hadn't knocked on any doors. Was Connie one of those people who talk a good game but don't follow through? Was she one of those people you can't count on? I remember thinking those things, but I had to wonder why she kept coming back. It had to be a little embarrassing, always reporting what she did not do. My first reaction was to ask someone else to do Connie's section and move on, hoping she would eventually drop out so that her inaction would not dull the others' enthusiasm. Dumb idea. Glad I didn't act on it. Without really thinking, I just asked, "What can you do?" "I can type," she responded. "Maybe I could do a newsletter." It turned out that she could do a number of other things in addition to putting out a good newsletter. A year later she was president of the organization.

Everybody can do something. If nothing else, they can just show up. Usually there is something else. What you want people to do may not be what they think they can do. Instead of irritating each other, why don't you just find out what they think they can do and have them do it? In addition to any special talent or the ability to perform routine work, every person knows someone else. Among those contacts are people who have money or influence, or simply the ability to spread the word about the organization. When you believe that everyone has something to contribute, you will find ways to make contributing easy. When members treat each other as contributors, an attitude of mutual value develops, and contributions instinctively occur.

It is not just the special few. Everyone has something to offer.

 # Recognizing the Roles of Acceptance and Confidence

To some extent, each change effort causes people to engage their incompetence. No matter how often we have been involved in change efforts, we have never been in this particular change, with its unique circumstances. Thus, we are always on the edge of knowing what to do. Those who have little experience in working for change may feel themselves even farther from that edge. At the same time, however, they need to gain acceptance from a new set of people or acceptance as competent in a new role from the people they know.

Even when encountering the opposition, you need to take the feelings of acceptance and regard into account as you consider your tactics.

This set of rules helps you understand that concerns over acceptance and confidence occur and that they can influence how people act in a change episode.

People want to be accepted and liked

Continued involvement in work for change may have as much to do with the very human needs for being accepted and liked as they do with concern over the issue itself. You can bet that many of the people who drop out of a change effort do so because they felt unwelcome or unimportant. A surprising number will get their feelings hurt without letting anyone know directly. You don't voluntarily spend much time in places where people do not like you. Neither will members of an organization.

Don't take for granted that people know they are accepted and liked. You may have to let them know. Using people's names and purposefully including them in simple conversations are easy steps that will pay off. Resist the temptation to form a special in-group within your organization. In-groups create out-groups.

People need to feel worthy and able, competent and confident

Most of us hold back a little when we are not sure how to do something, and most of us don't commit to something that we don't think is going to work. If we continue to find ourselves in a position where we just don't feel capable, we will probably try to find ourselves a new place to be. Insecurity is debilitating.

In contrast, when we are pretty sure of ourselves, we are much more comfortable. It is energizing to be part of something that seems to be working. When we feel competent and confident, we are much more willing to take risks, and little setbacks don't bother us so much. Confidence confers poise in the face of adversity. Not only do we like to feel this way about ourselves but we like to be recognized for our worth and abilities. When we know that others regard us as having value, it becomes easier for us to act in a valuable way. In any situation it feels much better to be seen as a contributor than to be seen as needy or not seen at all.

One of the most important sets of actions you can take as a change agent is to promote members' mutual recognition of each other's value and abilities while helping to develop the competence and confidence of those working with you. Do this in a conscious way. You will find that members will contribute more, take on more responsibilities, initiate more, and be willing to take up the slack. Disappointments will be much easier to take, and conflicts among members will be reduced. Increased competence and confidence will lead to a greater willingness to provide new leadership, which is so critical to an organization's success.

People become more competent through practice, so members of an organization should have the chance to do things. Mistakes should be expected and accepted as part of the deal. They should be met with encouragement and used to increase learning.

Confidence is associated with an anticipation of success. This is fostered by an awareness of successes already achieved. Consequently, members will need to notice results and see their own and the organization's progress.

Both insecurity and confidence are infectious. Insecurity may be more naturally present in a new enterprise. Confidence may need a little more nurturing.

People need acknowledgment more than they need agreement

People need to be heard and understood, and they need to know that this has occurred. Genuine acknowledgment of a person's ideas and interests affirms the individual's very existence. It is a way of confirming a connection between people, and it recognizes that they are an accepted part of the community, whether that be a family or a village. Acknowledging a person's right to be heard and considered acknowledges her or his right to be here. This takes place when you link your understanding with their intent to be understood. Such an action reduces the tension that flows from feeling disconnected, from feeling outside or less than.

Agreement certainly feels good, but it is less fundamental. Agreement is the second step and must be preceded by acknowledgment. Furthermore, agreements that appear to be based on a lack of honest understanding, whether that is real or perceived, can be interpreted as dismissive.

To matter matters.

People need to save face

What does it feel like to be seen as stupid or incompetent, especially in front of other people? What is it like to make a foolish mistake and to have that publicly pointed out to you by someone you don't particularly like? How would you like to be embarrassed?

You may become very defensive when your shortcomings are pointed out to you. Inadequacy or weakness are feelings you probably want to avoid. If the tactics you are using to make changes raise these feelings in other people, what response are you likely to get?

Too often I have seen groups seemingly bent on humiliating another party. They are determined to show that another is wrong. Why put someone through this? If you force someone to admit to some failing as a condition of his or her agreement with you, it is likely that you will have a tough time making that agreement.

Your goals probably have something to do with changing a policy or bringing some new activity to life. Rarely is your goal to diminish another, yet it may be tempting to get sidetracked in this direction. What you have to do is secure a change. Most often you don't necessarily have to show that someone is wrong.

Although normally you do not need to belittle, there may be times when discrediting another individual or organization is appropriate. You may need to eliminate or weaken an opponent that you will likely face again. Perhaps it will be important to expose hypocrisy or mismanagement. It could be important to bring down one adversary as an example to others. Or maybe your organization needs the emotional uplift of defeating a bully. In cases such as these, humbling another party would be an important, intended outcome directly related to accomplishment of your goals. This is quite different from being careless or arrogant.

When you back someone into a corner with few options, he or she will fight you. People will do some pretty irrational things to save face. So, unless there is some compelling reason to do otherwise, avoid making someone look foolish, incompetent, or wrong. It is much more effective to give your opponent an out. Find some way your opponent can save face while agreeing with you. This should be part of your planning, because it will certainly be part of theirs.

 ## Recognize Common Human Traits That Must Be Taken Into Account

You can expect people to act as people generally do, even though you may imagine your partners to be more admirable and your opponents more mysterious. This set of rules invites you to pay attention to some very practical concerns.

People hear selectively and remember what suits them

You have taken a box of rigatoni off the supermarket shelf, comparing it to the penne pasta you're holding in your other hand. The penne loses, and you put it back amid what seems like at least 73 other types of pasta. Now you become aware of the grocery store music, a catchy tune you have hummed along with a few times before. You can hear the music. It fits with something you know. Funny what you tune in and tune out.

Most of us pick up on things that fit. The things that make sense to us are those things that attach themselves to other things that already make sense to us. We seem to be more receptive to information, ideas, and emotions that conform to the beliefs or suspicions we hold in situations in which there are a range of alternative opinions. This provides us with a little security, a little confidence, a little more assurance that we are right.

Now, the messages we extract and value are not always the messages that were intended to be sent. We do a little selecting and some reconfiguring, trying to make sense of things. Information is like colored tile laying scattered at our feet. We pick up a little red one here, a blue one there. The yellow one seems a bit big, but we like the color, so we break off a smaller part and throw the rest away. We turn each piece this way and that until we find where it fits in the mosaic we are constructing that represents our view of the world. Things that don't fit or don't look right don't go in the mosaic.

We are not bad people to do this, and we don't do this all the time. Sometimes we reshape our design, but rarely do we reject it altogether. It is just that what we want to be true is important to us, so we look for evidence of confirmation. If our truths seem to be under attack, we may very well grab more frantically, sometimes splintering things into pretty odd shapes just to make them fit.

A friend of mine went sailing. He didn't want to be lost, but he was. He certainly did not want to admit to his semi-trusting passenger that he was lost, so he started interpreting landmarks in a way that told him he was on course. The way this island was shaped or this channel ran conformed with how he wanted them to be. Needless to say—but I'll say it anyway—he ended up far from where he'd hoped to be. When do you alter your perceptions to fit the reality you want?

What about what we remember? Events are more harrowing or heroic; offenses and slights are exaggerated. Mistakes (on our part) are minimized or well explained. Most of us tend to re-create history to serve our present purposes.

Expect people to do this. It is natural. It may need to be confronted, but it shouldn't be denied. And remember, when you do confront, you are probably engaged in a similar adventure yourself.

People need to feel connected with others yet prized for their uniqueness

The individual member of a group draws support, protection, and assistance from involvement with others. At the same time, the member wants to act alone and unencumbered. Wanting to be recognized; wanting to blend in. Well, which is it? The individual wants the name the group can offer, but also wants a name within it. This is the dance of the human condition, one that has some curious and at times unpredictable steps.

Understand then that each member of the group, including you, will on occasion be looking to join while at other times acting to differentiate. This process varies among individuals and cultures, but some degree of these apparently opposite desires resides in each of us. Learn how to dance.

People want freedom and direction, simultaneously

Another variation of the dance. "Leave me alone" and "Tell me what to do" can almost be uttered in the same sentence. You can interpret this in a number of ways. For example, this may mean leave me alone while I figure out how to do what you tell me to do. Or, give me a general idea, but let me do it my way. Or, I want some guidance, but I don't want you clucking around like a mother hen. Or even, let me do it my way and blame it on you if it doesn't work. There are any number of variations.

Without this tension between freedom and dependence there would be no chance for individuals to develop their own capabilities and no opportunity to learn from others. Those who are likely to be your best emerging leaders will struggle most with this conundrum. Avoid demanding that anyone make an either/or choice. Pay attention to the rhythm.

People can see only what their vantage point allows them to see

Vantage points are shaped by values, interests, and experiences. We are particularly keen to recognize those things that touch our self-interests. When you open the newspaper, what do you look for first? Some people check the stock market, some the want ads, some the local news. Others find out what Congress has been up to, and more than a few go right to the box scores. Hardly any two people will read the articles in the newspaper in precisely the same way.

Because of our experiences, we expect to see certain things in the places we look. Because of our experiences, we predict not only what we will see but what will happen as well. Experience, values, and interests all work to reinforce each other, creating a code we use to interpret the world around us. This, then, also becomes part of our experience.

My mom couldn't believe that I could walk into the kitchen and not notice that the garbage needed to be taken out. Garbage toting was a critical daily contribution I was expected to make to the smooth and healthful running of our household. Searching for an afternoon snack from the fridge, I would be drawn to the kitchen. Looking at the remains of last night's dinner in the garbage hardly ever occurred to me. "Can't you see it needs emptying" was her almost daily refrain. Actually, no, I couldn't.

Patient woman, my mother. Over time her invitations to see if the garbage needed emptying took hold. I did want to do a good job, and certain matters of self-interest were affected by my ability to remember to look for the garbage. It took a while, but the necessary glance toward the receptacle finally became incorporated into my experience. Now, many years later, I can readily see when the garbage needs to be taken out. Why can't my daughters see it?

I bet there are some things you just don't notice with the same frequency or importance as do others, who may be mystified at your blindness—the general condition of the bathroom or the level of oil on the dipstick, for example. There are also hunger, sexism, pollution, child abuse, alienation, and a host of other things that some would believe it impossible to miss while others find it impossible to see.

It may take a while longer than what may seem reasonable, but people can recognize when things are becoming unhealthy. They can learn to take care of the garbage.

People are open to influence when they are distracted

When you are distracted, your judgment and your interest are off running around with the subject of your distraction. You more easily defer to the judgment and interest that are more available, which would be the judgment and interest of the party asking for your decision or approval. You are not really paying attention.

There are all sorts of distractions. You may, for example, be distracted by the power of another or by your wish not to appear foolish. You may be worried about how to pay this month's rent, or how to keep your son in school. You could find yourself in a situation in which many interests vie for your attention. Your concern over your own immediate interests may make you vulnerable to a deal that harms your interests over the long run or harms the interests of your neighbor.

In each of these situations you bring less to the discussion than the other party. You may rely on what they present because it makes more sense than any argument you can muster. You may make a decision just so you can turn your attention back to the source of your distraction.

This could be a problem within your organization. People may not remember agreements they made while distracted. As a result, they may not follow through on important assignments, or they may question an apparently agreed-upon course of action. This is one of those "where were you when we talked about this" experiences. You can reduce problems by making sure that decisions are clear and understood, but you need to accept the fact that you probably won't prevent them altogether.

Distraction can be used as a tactic to get a favorable and quick agreement out of an opponent. You can create new distractions or draw attention to preoccupations that already exist. Your opponent will concentrate less well on the subject at hand while you are well prepared to make your case.

Whether or not you have intentionally exploited the situation, be aware that agreements made during moments of distraction are weak agreements, ones in which the other party has a reduced investment. If the other party does not have much interest in the issue and all you need is some sort of approval rather than cooperation, this may not matter. If mutual interest in the issue is high or you need an actual commitment, incentives for keeping the agreement in place may be needed. Also, be aware that distraction is a tactic that can be used against you. For more on this topic, see the work of Johnson and Johnson (1997), listed in the recommended readings at the end of the book.

People are less open to influence when they have been inoculated against it

Go out on the street. Look up and down as far as you can see. Go to the top of the tallest building around and stretch your eyes toward the horizon. The earth is flat. No doubt about it. Except for a few peaks and valleys, the earth is flat. You can see it with your own eyes. Do you believe this?

Before you ever seriously thought about whether the earth was round or flat or just one huge pyramid, somebody got to you. Probably some leftist teacher in grade school. They may have even shown you pictures from some space mission. Pretty powerful stuff. You believe those words and those pictures, but you don't believe your own eyes.

New information doesn't take if you have been inoculated against it. If you have been given information that you believe is true or even possibly true, you will at least be skeptical about information that doesn't coincide with it. Let's say you are given a set of facts and statistics to support a point of view. The more you believe this information, the less willing you will be to accept an argument that tries to get you to support a different point of view.

Telling someone in advance that they will be subject to an influence attempt is a way of making the attempt less successful. For example, if someone tells you that a salesperson will use a particular line on you to get you to buy a product, that line will be unconvincing when you hear it.

The vast middle ground of the uncommitted is sought by the various parties in a dispute. A sort of propaganda battle ensues. For the sake of this discussion, let's assume there is a side for truth and justice and that you are on it. You do need to take the propaganda issue seriously. You will succeed more easily if you use inoculation techniques rather than trying to counter a message that has already been delivered. You can inoculate a group against misleading information by presenting accurate information in advance in a clearly understandable way. You can strengthen inoculation and preempt an opponent's line by letting people know the line is coming. A simple "this is what you are going to be told" will have a strong effect. Then you can point out the flaws in the information or reasoning contained in the opposing propaganda. It is very difficult for propaganda to influence a group of people who have been inoculated against it.

People don't like to think their time is being wasted, especially by someone else

"Get to the point!" you would yell if you were not nearly as polite as you are. The meeting is going nowhere. The only constant seems to be that each comment leads to the distraction of yet another side issue. Two hours later the thing comes to a merciful end with little accomplished save an agreement to repeat this nonsense all over again in two weeks.

As you are leaving, you hear an exasperated "what a waste of time" uttered soft enough to almost qualify for under the breath status but loud enough that at least half a dozen people could hear. You are ready to shake your head in agreement when you notice the person uttering the remark is the same guy whose meaningless commentary consumed a good deal of the time he claims was wasted. You really do shake your head now, from side to side.

How can someone be so oblivious? There are those of us, like this fellow, who tend to think that what we have to say is so valuable that all within earshot will treasure its educational if not its entertainment value. Then there are those, like the organizers of that meeting, who asked others to take part in an activity, believing that the activity itself had some intrinsic worth. Basically these individuals have overvalued the benefit of their actions and requests relative to the worth of others' time. Any irritation stems from undervaluing the benefit of others' actions relative to the worth of their own time. That is, they have valued their interests but have not valued the interests of others.

You probably feel your time is wasted if the outcome you expected from your investment of time was not produced or if the outcome required much more investment of time than you had expected. Maybe you have to go to five different stores to get some item you thought the first store should have. Perhaps you sit down in front of the computer for a whole afternoon and still can't get the thing to do what you want.

You might even attend a 2-hour meeting that doesn't achieve what you had hoped.

Remember this relationship of outcome, investment, and expectation. You need to have a clear sense that the outcome intended by the investment of time will be sufficiently valuable to those making the investment. If you haven't given much thought to the intended outcome, or to the investment you are asking for, you may well have people feeling that their time has been wasted. It's bad enough when the choices you make about the use of your time do not produce the desired result. But it's even more irritating when the choices someone else makes about your time produce nothing of value to you.

Under stress people may vent their frustrations on the nearest available object

The nearest available object might be a person, even a friend. The use of the word "object" is purposeful. In these circumstances the recipient of the expressed frustration loses special identity or value. The transfer of frustration to some other point becomes more important than the object itself.

When pressure is high, people's fuses are short. Patience is hard to maintain when time is limited or the stakes are high. Arguments among members become more likely, and attitudes become more critical. If you talk about these matters before pressure mounts, shared awareness of this tendency may prevent or reduce its occurrence. If frustration was to boil over, members would at least be forewarned and not taken aback so by the event. They would be better able to deal with the challenge.

Don't be surprised if you are the object of some frustration during a tense moment. The criticism may be more about the feelings of tension than about you. Don't be surprised if you find yourself tempted to make someone else an object. How will you handle that?

All human behavior is designed to meet needs and is purposeful, not accidental

All behavior is purposeful, even behavior that seems a little odd. You might not know what another's purpose is. Neither might they, but there are clues. Look at what is being produced, not just at what is being done. What is someone getting or trying to get from his or her actions?

Actions usually involve one of the basic needs—inclusion, control, affection, recognition, creativity, pleasure, accomplishment, or altruism.

Your opponents and your allies alike will all be acting in ways that make good sense. Start with that understanding. If their actions or reactions don't make sense to you, one of two things is probably taking place. You may be assuming a set of needs that are different from those being acted on. Or you may be aware of a possible set of responses to the situation that the other party does not see or considers impossible.

Once you take a look at things from the point of view of the other party meeting their needs, not yours, things become a little clearer. Even though you understand their behavior a little better, you still might want to change it. If you want people to act in a different way, you will have to introduce a new set of more important needs or offer new ways to meet existing needs. These are your fundamental choices. It gets more complicated, of course.

Knowing what to do doesn't necessarily tell you how to do it. Planned change requires a little thinking and a new set of actions on your part as you develop and implement strategies and tactics around the fundamental choices you make. Just shaking your head will probably be insufficient.

Recognizing Matters That Lead to Inaction

Since action is the essential ingredient in producing change, it is helpful to consider the factors that lead to inaction. A number of very understandable conditions keep people from acting effectively. This set of rules helps you recognize those barriers to action.

Fear of losing what has been granted by those in power can lead people to docility

"Don't complain or they'll take away the little that we've got." I bet you have heard sentiments like that before. You don't give the Food Stamp office a hard time. You shut up and put up with bad working conditions. The social service agency you work for doesn't complain about the United Way that gives you money.

These are all legitimate responses to fear, and they illustrate the power differences that persist when people remain unorganized and dependent. In this situation people have no evident alternative to the power that holds them hostage. They hope to keep those in power happy by keeping quiet about their own unhappiness. Instead of inviting others to join with them to build power, they ask others to join them in silent misery. "Don't complain."

I agree. Organize.

When people are confused, they say no

Three phone calls, one right after the other, and you thought you were going to catch a little TV tonight. Everybody seems to be asking you to do something. First, someone you don't know very well asks you to work for a political candidate you are not sure about. You've heard a couple of people say he supports the right things, but wasn't he involved in that insurance scandal a few years back? He just seems so slick. Not 10 seconds after you hang up the phone, your buddy calls with some great new investment deal for you, but he's pretty fuzzy on the details. The phone rings again, and it's somebody from work. Seems like a few people have been talking, and they want you to go with them to the boss to confront her about the "sorry state of affairs around here." You're not quite sure what they mean, and they don't seem to have any specific complaints.

Which of these requests did you say yes to? Any? If you are like most people, you said no to all three. Commitment requires sufficient understandable justification. If people aren't pretty sure which way to go, they won't go anywhere. Asking people to become involved with your change effort, to make some sort of commitment, must acknowledge this fact. If the problem or the nature of the benefit is not clear to them, you will not get much of a commitment. Commitment will grow as clarity increases.

This principle also applies when your group is faced with a decision. Those who want the group to go in a particular direction sometimes push for a decision before other members of the group are ready. This usually results in some degree of group dissension, often behind-the-back grumbling dissension. People feel pressured. They may say they'll agree with the decision, but they don't commit to it. Those who favor the decision become irritated that others don't seem to be doing much to support the new direction and the group starts to splinter into camps.

Avoid prematurely moving your group to a decision. You can tell when you are doing this, and you will just have to pull back for a moment until the group is really able to decide. Just because something is clear to you does not mean it is clear or easily understood by other people. All groups need some degree of risk taking, but moving ahead when there is too strong a climate of uncertainty will probably backfire.

Finally, this notion can work in your favor. If you are trying to defeat something that requires community support, you may not have to get people to agree with you. You may need only to stir up confusion. This is a favorite tactic of those who wish to defeat a ballot proposition. They put forward a couple of competing propositions that are somewhat similar. The resulting confusion keeps any one proposition from getting the necessary support.

If you want to halt or stall something, create confusion. If you want commitment, create clarity.

People run out of gas

Long meetings, long struggle, long hours devoted to completing a project—so long. People cannot sustain interest and activity indefinitely. Although recognition of progress can add energy, people need other things. They need breaks. They need diversions. They need to clear their heads. They need an extra boost now and then.

Even though change agents know that people run out of gas, they tend to act like this isn't true. Sometimes we try to get as much as we can out of people before they become exhausted rather than helping them to fill up the tank from time to time.

Pay attention to the need for people to gas up—change the nature of their responsibilities, have some fun, and give them a little rest. Even when you take these and other steps to maintain involvement, don't be surprised to see people who have been very active taper off a bit. Some are taking a self-imposed break to be followed by a renewed level of activity. Others will becoming less active, and still others will fade away altogether, sometimes rather abruptly. This will happen. It is hard for most people to maintain a consistently high level of activity. Accept this fact. Be appreciative of the contributions individuals have made, and allow for the lower level of participation they may now need.

People are intimidated by the prospect of having to do it all

Becoming involved seems somehow to imply a responsibility for solving the problem—all of it—and that's a pretty big job. Although members understand that others are involved, there is still a tendency to think that "I" am building the recreation center or stopping the rape of the desert or getting the school to offer parenting classes to teenage dads. We know this isn't really the case, but this feeling of being swamped will weigh some members down and discourage others from participating at all.

Participants need to understand the goal of the effort, but they also must be able to clearly see their role and the role of others. Members do need to feel the problem, but they do not need to take sole ownership of it. They only need to own their own piece of it. You may need to remind each other of this occasionally to bring each person's involvement down to a manageable size.

People find security in their routines

Some people won't go to Mexico. Beautiful beaches, lush tropical forests, and breathtaking canyons all await the visitor, still, some won't go. "I ain't gonna cross that border. Nope. No way. They talk funny, and all the people down there are foreigners."

Routines create a kind of boundary line that some people are unable to cross. Routines are very powerful. People don't like to break them. They are safe. They are known. You confront this reality when you work for change.

Don't be too disappointed if some of the people who seem to agree with you don't back up their words with any action. Even going to a meeting may mean missing the current "most talked about" evening drama series or Monday Night Football. The daily predictability of established patterns has been well learned. A new set of patterns, creating a new, if only temporary, routine, may not seem worth the effort. Over time, some resistant people will slowly join you, inching into the water as they adjust to the temperature. Others won't.

Sometimes when you get a large enough group of people who seem to know their way, a few newcomers will decide to brave the border and join you in the Mexican sunshine. A lot of others will still just ask you to bring them back some tequila.

Lots of people will not ask for help

People who are new to the organization or those who need to appear to be experts or very well organized have difficulty asking for help. Groups that create norms that legitimize asking for help are more productive. Still, new members haven't been acculturated to these norms, and certain experts often feel above them.

It is usually evident when someone is having difficulty fulfilling a responsibility. Knowing that they can ask for help may not make much of a difference. Some people just don't ask. An offer to help can reduce tension and reinforce collaborative norms. Waiting too long for someone to request assistance may result in losing that person altogether. Members need to get into the habit of offering help as well as asking for it.

Helping someone is different from substituting your work for theirs. Helping means that you do things with people, not for them.

 ## Getting People Moving Toward Action and Keeping Them Going

Now that you have considered inaction, think about the things that do lead to action. This set of rules helps you recognize how you might make use of those factors that provide motivation.

If people cannot feel anything, they won't do anything

It is not enough just to know. You know many things that you don't act on. Things that you should act on, but don't. Floss. Eat less salt. Keep your checkbook balanced. You act out of discomfort, joy, anger, excitement, or some other emotion, not out of knowledge. Your awareness of the need for gas turns to action when the needle scratches the "E." Your desire to read textbooks increases when you are excited about the subject or when a test is a few hours away. When do you decide to take a stand, join a group, or spend less money?

People have to feel something about the issue, not just know about it. Education is helpful, but it is insufficient for action. Your efforts to get people involved in working for change must touch some emotion. An organization that has no emotion is lifeless. Get people irritated. Get them angry. Get them excited. That is how you will get and keep people going.

Fear of the discomfort of disappointment can be more powerful than discomfort with the present situation

To try something and to fail hurts. The higher the stakes, the more it hurts. If you have ever watched the losing bench in a championship game—high school, college, or pros—the pain is there, visible. The body can't seem to hold it. It leaks down the faces and slumps the shoulders with its weight. And these are the people who are better than everyone else except one other team. They are next to first, not next to last.

You will run across people who do not want to risk this pain, even when the stakes aren't all that high. They may not like their current circumstances, but this is a dull, accustomed discomfort spread out over time. To raise and then lose hope is more difficult than not allowing for hope at all.

In most cases of community change there is not one winner with everyone else a loser. In most cases you gain something, often along with other people who have different immediate interests. On occasion you will be able to demonstrate to some of the reluctant that it is not an all-or-nothing predicament. It will take a long time for them to see that, and some may not be able to see it at all.

You will encounter different forms of resistance from those who would benefit from the changes being proposed. Some of these will be a surprise to you. Some will make you angry. The better you are at understanding the things that get in people's way, the better you will be at devising ways to get around those barriers. You will also learn when not to beat your head against a wall.

People need to be sufficiently uncomfortable or sufficiently excited before they will take action

There is little reason to put energy into changing a situation that you find acceptable, especially if the alternative is not all that attractive. However, as the gap between attractiveness of the current situation and the attractiveness of a new situation grows, so does interest in working for change. As a change agent, you need to work on that gap.

It is usually easier to start by intensifying dissatisfaction with current circumstances. People are more willing and able to consider something different once they have become restless or unhappy with what they have right now. If you are satisfied with your job, you are not going to put much time into looking for a new one. The same holds true for your apartment, your car, or the place you buy your groceries. When you begin to grow tired of any of these or when irritations begin exceeding satisfactions, you begin to look around.

As a change agent, you might poke and irritate and foment until people are so aggravated that they are ready to replace what they have with anything that looks different. Then you will be ready to introduce an alternative. The more attractive and more possible the alternative the better. You shift to building enthusiasm for a new direction, and assist the community to clearly identify what that will be.

Throughout the life of the change episode, you will need to keep that gap intact or widen it by calling attention to areas of bitterness and to prospects of a different and appealing better condition. That tension is a source of energy that will continue to fuel the group's efforts.

People need to believe in the possibility of a successful outcome to take action

If you do not believe your actions will produce the desired outcome, you will not take action. You will avoid a math class if you do not think you will pass. You will not run for mayor if you think nobody will notice. You will not seriously go shopping for a Lexus when the best you can do is save up for a skateboard.

Unless they are totally desperate, people presented with an opportunity to work for change will do nothing if they don't believe they have a chance to succeed. One of your challenges will be to keep success in sight, to make it seem real and within reach. To do this you may need to redefine success. Present success as a series of smaller accomplishments, and note the realization of each.

People tend to take things more seriously when they are accountable to other people

When people are working to complete a task, the nature of the work itself and its importance provides motivation. The simple fact that someone has decided to do something implies a goal. This creates a tension between the current level of completion and whatever "finished" might be. Accountability to another adds yet another incentive. Accountability adds relationship, and maintaining that relationship requires that you work in an effective and timely manner.

You do this all the time yourself. At your job you do your work because it's important, but also because your boss expects you to. You delivered those campaign brochures throughout your neighborhood because you support the candidate, but also because someone from the campaign staff is going to call to see if you did. Your apartment probably looks a little cleaner an hour before company arrives than it did in the morning.

Members of your organization may agree to do a job because it's important, but important may be insufficient for getting the job done.

People perform tasks, but to some extent they perform for other people as well. If you can build some type of accountability into the assignments people take on, you will undoubtedly see an increase in productivity. Accountability should not be heavy-handed. Some simple method of reporting progress or completion can be enough. The more specific your accountability methods are, the better. That is, being accountable to a specific person or a specific team within the organization is better than general accountability to the overall membership.

Knowing that your work matters to you will help you do it well. Knowing that it also matters to someone else may help you do it better. This implies no shortcoming on your part. It is simply that the added dimension of some sort of relationship contributes to productivity.

People tend to wait until the last minute to get things done

It is the deadline that makes the task real. The things you have to do seem less interesting simply because you have to do them. This little loss of freedom creates a little resistance. So you put assignments off while you do things you want to do. Or you do those things you have put off until now. Lots of things get in the way of doing the things you have to do.

If the assignments in your organization do not get partnered with a completion date, you can do a lot of waiting. The date helps to bring the matter to the top of the list so it can get the attention it needs. Having some system of reminders, like using a Nag, helps to keep dates from getting forgotten. Deadlines should be realistic, but they should also be specified a little earlier than absolutely necessary to give you a margin of safety.

People need to see immediate results to keep going

This rule applies especially to those less identified with the issues and the goals of the organization. Those who have initiated the effort or who feel keenly about the need for change will continue to invest their energy and hope over a longer period of time before they need to see a payoff. Those less convinced of the need for action or its prospects for success must see that some of the work has an immediate effect, either in the form of noticeable progress toward a changed condition or in producing an increased number of participants.

Some of these individuals won't ever be sufficiently pleased. If you find that you are frequently trying to talk someone into remaining involved, stop talking. This person will never be satisfied enough to make a significant contribution anyway. The energy you spend trying to keep an individual only nominally in the fold is better spent doing other work, like recruiting new members. Although the ambivalent may drop out of the effort, a few will reappear once the bandwagon has really begun to move.

Newer members of the organization generally fall into the category of the uncertain. They may have waited until they sensed you were real before joining, or they have just become aware of the cause. In either case they probably need to see some evidence that the work is having an impact.

The more a person becomes identified with the endeavor, the more patient he or she will become. However, remember that all participants will eventually need to recognize signs of progress to keep the faith.

People relate far better to a problem with which they have had a direct, personal experience

"Teachers have it easy. School's out in the afternoon, and they get all that vacation. They spend all their time around children, so they don't have to deal with the hassles of the real world." My guess is that whoever holds this opinion never spent much time facing a classroom.

Those who have children with special health care needs understand the difficulties much more than those who don't. Victims of domestic violence have felt the pain more intensely than those who have only read about it. And it's a lot easier to get you and your three kids off welfare if you have never been on it. Experience teaches.

It is sometimes difficult to really get hold of an issue that lives only in the abstract for you. You may grasp it at an intellectual level without really having it touch you. Does this mean that you should not get involved with an issue you have not experienced? No. Change requires the involvement of a range of interested parties. What this does mean, however, is that those who have experienced the issue need to have some decision-making authority over the direction the action to resolve the issue will take.

This seems self-evident, doesn't it? In many situations this if fairly easy to accomplish because the people who feel the problem have initiated responses to change it. In other circumstances, however, one group, often some set of professionals, works to make changes to benefit another set of people (for example, consumers of social services). Very often they work on behalf of, not along side of, these intended beneficiaries. How often are clients and other recipients of services involved in working to promote change? How often are they in decision-making rather than advisory roles?

In some instances those who have experienced a particular problem may keenly relate to it but may not want to take action on it. There are many barriers to involvement. Some may want to avoid the social stigma that acknowledging their experience would bring. Others may want to distance themselves from the pain of the problem, which may involve distancing themselves from efforts to work toward its resolution. A few barriers deal with current levels of ability. Many of those who have direct experience spend so much time dealing with the day-to-day aspects of the problem that they do not have much energy left over to deal with broader matters. Others may lack an understanding of the political aspects of the system needing change. Few of those who have been personally affected may have developed the necessary leadership skills a change effort requires.

You will probably face all of these impediments in your attempt to meaningfully involve those who depend on some sort of service in working for change. Be aware of the barriers to equal participation and discover ways to overcome them.

In addition to these practical matters, ethical issues must be confronted. Who should have power and control? Whose discomfort is least acceptable? Whose is most acceptable? Ethical issues such as these need to be acknowledged and explored.

When organizing to promote change, understand that some of your most committed participants will be those who have had a firsthand experience with the issue. Actively recruit these individuals, knowing that in some cases you will need to overcome some very practical barriers to their participation.

To take action you need people; to get people you need action; changes result from the actions of people

The whole business of community change is about people. People do things, and the things they do attract other people who begin doing things themselves. These actions are intended to produce responses from other people. It is all about people and what they do. The more you accustom yourself to learning about people, the greater your chance for success.

What you know about people will never be completely sufficient or completely correct. Keep learning and testing what you have learned.

PART III

Putting It All Together

CHAPTER **7**

The Thirteen Commandments

The Thirteen Commandments are the core rules, if you will. They represent the fundamental precepts for promoting change and have stood the tests of time and action. Whenever I get stuck, I look to these things first. Observe the Thirteen Commandments and you will be amply rewarded.

1. Thou Shalt Hustle

Don't sit still. Pay attention. Anticipate. Get there quicker. Seize the moment. Take advantage of any opening. Get things for free or real cheap. Get in the game.

"Hustle" has many meanings. It is a good verb to learn and a good habit to practice. When you hustle, you think two or three steps ahead. You put yourself in position to capitalize on the actions and reactions taking place around you. Relax and enjoy life, certainly. But when you do commit yourself to action, give yourself fully to that decision.

2. Thou Shalt Keep the Cycle of Empowerment Rolling

Build your power through the cycle of action, involvement, communication, decision, and new action. The power of the individual and the power of the group must grow and accelerate.

Everything revolves around people acting powerfully. To do this people must build relationships and use their power wisely and effectively. The power directed toward an issue must always be greater than the power of the issue. Therefore, groups must continue to build their power if they intend to take on more significant issues.

Pay attention to each element in the cycle of empowerment to generate power and continue progressing. The use of power demands ethical strength, whether to comply, to collaborate, or to overcome.

3. Thou Shalt Do Thy Homework

You cannot act effectively in ignorance. The more you know about your community, your issue, your supporters, your strategies, and any opposition you face, the more focused and productive your actions will be.

Information is a resource. You will never know everything, so don't wait until you know everything to act. However, you can find out many things if you take the time to look. If you do not, you will waste time on ineffective action or on repairing damage that could have been prevented.

Homework, finding things out, is part of the necessary preparation for action. Use action to gather more information.

4. Thou Shalt Hit Them in Their Self-Interest

People respond more quickly and purposefully to things that prick their self-interest than to anything else. These are spots of sensitivity and vulnerability. This is true for both supporters and opponents.

Hitting them in their self-interest is not necessarily exploitive, but it certainly can be. The most effective actions occur when individual goals are matched with group goals, or when the interests of one segment of the community are met in a way that meets the overall interests of the community. This alignment of interests reduces resistance and promotes positive movement. You cannot act to achieve mutual benefit if you have no idea what would benefit the other party.

You can manipulate perceptions of a situation so that it would appear that the interests of a party are being met when in fact they are not. This, in my view, would be exploitive. Whether or not that is ethical is left to your assessment of the legitimate interests of the parties involved and the range of options for action.

Sometimes individuals and groups act before they have fully considered what could be in their best interests. We all act short-sighted from time to time, and we may react rather than reflect. Take time to examine the fundamental interests of the key players. Directing your attention to the interests of those affected by current conditions or a changed situation will direct your actions.

5. Thou Shalt Have Those Who Feel the Problem Play a Significant Role in Solving the Problem

Only in rare cases should you act for someone instead of with them. These exceptions—for example, acting on behalf of infants—occur when the beneficiaries of action are truly incapable of acting on their own behalf. If you act for others rather than with them, you promote dependency and increase the imbalance of power. There is a bit of arrogance in assuming that you know better than someone else about their conditions.

In many cases those who are to benefit from an action do have relatively little power and few skills in community change. Although this should be accepted as the initial condition, it should not be accepted as a permanent condition. Expecting people to act on their own interests to the best of their ability connotes dignity. Assisting them to do so demonstrates belief in dignity.

Those who feel the problem have insights and information that others can have in only a limited form, if at all. This knowledge is critical for effective action. The designers of action cannot adequately understand what needs to take place if those who have crucial information are left out of the design and the implementation.

Action is more likely to be sustained when those who are directly affected are involved in leadership. The enthusiasm of other parties will wane as their interest is drawn elsewhere. The interests of those most directly affected will remain.

6. Thou Shalt Allow the Situation to Dictate the Strategy

Any strategy can be effective given the right circumstance. Given the wrong circumstance, any strategy can be a failure. The circumstance decides, not the strategy.

Formulate your strategy by identifying the opportunities and the risks in the situation. Avoid entering with a preconceived way for approaching things. Collaboration is not always readily possible, and confrontation will not always work. Pursuing your pet approach may serve your style, but it may not meet the requirements of the situation you face. Test and modify strategies until you hit on the approach that best fits the current situation.

Do what works and what is ethical. It is not ethical to do what doesn't work.

7. Thou Shalt Have a Quick Initial Victory

Immediately look for an opportunity to achieve a success. What can be done quickly and easily that will boost people's confidence in their abilities and the possibility of overall success?

A simple victory will get the ball rolling, establishing a positive momentum. One of the most important things you can do is to get a group unstuck and acting. There is almost always some simple action you can take to boost morale. It should be something fairly simple, not complicated or drawn out. Get people going with some form of active success. This lays the foundation for additional levels of involvement.

8. Thou Shalt Prevent Unintended Consequences

What will happen if we do this? That's a pretty important question to ask. What will happen if you attempt and fail? What will happen if you attempt and succeed? What unanticipated effects from your actions might you be able to anticipate if you stopped to think about things a bit?

Everything you do will have a ripple effect. The results of your action will continue to spread benefit far beyond your original intention, but sometimes this creates problems. Progress over here may mean some loss over there. Actions that are intended to please might offend a group you have overlooked.

Look beyond your present circumstances to see how your actions might be perceived by others outside your immediate circle or how the change you seek might affect other people's lives. Consider the consequences of your actions from a number of different viewpoints, but do this within reason. Remember that an inordinate fear of unintended consequences can lead to inaction. Just because something might happen does not mean that it is likely to happen. Think things through before you act, but keep your focus on action.

9. Thou Shalt Keep Thy Options Open

Every action should create other options, not reduce them. Even though you have committed to an action, prepare your plans so you can make changes and adjustments if necessary.

The more choices you have for action, the more you can determine what you will do. Keep testing until you find out what works. If you back yourself into a corner or sever your relationships with potential allies, you restrict your options and add strength to forces that are much less within your control.

Options create possibilities. Keep success possible.

10. Thou Shalt Do Things on Purpose

Every action you take should be matched with an intended outcome, otherwise it is quite possible that another outcome will be produced.

Too often groups are interested in what they want to do, not what they want to accomplish. The selection of your action flows from your prior selection of what it is that you want that action to produce. A critical question to ask is, "What do we want to have happen?" All actions will produce outcomes. Choosing an action without clearly identifying the intended outcome leaves the outcome more or less to chance.

Purposeful actions are related to a desired result, and they are born of a conscious decision. "We really didn't do it on purpose" means "We really did it thoughtlessly." Doing things purposefully is doing things thoughtfully. Purposeful action uses resources efficiently, effectively, and responsibly.

11. Thou Shalt Roll with the Punches

Despite all of your wonderfully purposeful planning, sometimes things won't work out. Due to cosmic interventions—flat tires, rain on your picnics, speaker malfunctions—your results may be disappointing. You can let these disappointments smack you in the face and knock you on your pockets—a strategy I personally think hurts too much—or you can look at what else you've got going for you or what else you can do. Roll with the punches.

The ability to roll with the punches is related to confidence. Your belief in your ability to manage despite setbacks will reduce the impact of those setbacks. A little perspective taking can come in handy too. If you define your experience narrowly in terms of your disappointment, you probably won't be the most pleasant person to be around. Broaden your perspective and acknowledge that some pretty satisfying things are happening as well.

You also need to ask yourself how big a deal this matter really is. If the situation does not present you with what you had expected, make the best of what it does present to you. In most cases you will still be able to make do, and the crisis of the moment will fade into a blurry history. A good sense of humor is a valuable asset to perspective taking.

Sometimes the crises are significant, and you just may need to accept the fact and move on. By believing that you can move on, you create a vision of alternative conditions you can bring about. Believe in yourself and in the other members of your group.

Much of the difficulty in handling complications is the unfounded belief that they won't occur. Of course, you know that they will, you just don't want to believe it. Hassles will get in the way, and things will go "kaflooey" now and again. It will happen. Handle it.

12. Thou Shalt Commit Thyself to Learning

A belief in learning is a belief in improvement. Things can always get better. Learning allows you to accept current conditions and current levels of effectiveness as temporary with a belief that you will be able to make them better. This is an empowering belief.

A person committed to learning can weather mistakes, their own and others. Mistakes are inevitable when we act in situations that are new to us. Our knowledge and our skills will occasionally come up short. Mistakes have to occur for us to learn. This orientation reduces inhibitions and empowers action.

Intelligence is not hiding your ignorance. No, it is actively searching it out and celebrating in its discovery. You can then replace ignorance with knowledge and skill.

When you decide to take the learning that each experience offers, everything you do leads to a chance to do it better. Learning becomes habit-forming. You begin to look at every situation as an opportunity for what it can teach you.

All organizations need to become more proficient. An organization committed to learning is purposeful and patient. It fosters a climate that encourages the learning of its members. Growth in leadership can only occur in the presence of opportunities to increase skill. The very attempt to learn becomes a key value in powerful organizations. In the most effective organizations, members are assisted with their learning so that unnecessary errors are minimized. The more skilled individuals guide those with less skill and in the process both gain.

A commitment to learning undermines a belief in failure. It promotes a belief in progress. Every experience, particularly the unexpected, is a rich source of learning. There is something there that you didn't know before. Find it.

13. Thou Shalt Laugh and PEA, and Thou Shalt Be Greatly Relieved

You have to be able to laugh, to take some delight in life. There is much to enjoy in the work that you do and in the company of others. Yes, there is misery in life, and there may well be pain and sorrow in the issues you are addressing. The constant company of misery, pain, and seriousness dulls the spirit and overinflates the ego. You are not so important that you cannot have a good time. Heck, from time to time get goofy. You see, after a while, people stop doing things they don't enjoy. Keep it enjoyable.

All right, what's this PEA business? Persistence. Energy. Action. You were thinking something else? If you forget all the rules except this one, you will still be successful more often than not. Of course, I think the other rules will increase your chances a bit. Still, if you remain persistent and don't give up, if you continue to develop and focus your energy, and if you take action, you will have accomplishments to celebrate.

And when you celebrate—laugh out loud.

The Rules of the Game

Acting to Change People's Interests

Those who play the game make the rules.

It's not "them."

People are the allies and the targets.

Any problem that involves more than just you will require more than just you to resolve it.

You don't have to involve everybody.

Turnover in leadership and membership is natural.

Human capital is the most valuable resource of any enterprise.

Each group needs a mainstay, someone who provides continuous assurance to other members.

Everything happens through relationships.

Things will be more important to you, the initiator, than to anyone else.

Countering Obstacles to Successful Action

The Rule of 33—things will be 33% different from your best guess.

Expect the ripple effects of change.

Unearned benefits accompany almost every successful change effort.

A religious experience may not last much past the prayer meeting— distractions of the "sinful" world usually prove too tempting.

Be wary of Sunday social activists and the sneeze experience.

Each community has its ankle weights, naysayers who need to drag down the unafraid.

The most powerful obstacles to change are fear, apathy, and ignorance.

Using Power Powerfully

You need a base of power equal to, if not greater than, the issue you face.

"Power with" is at least as important as "power over."

An effective change agent will help others discover and use their own power.

Fixing blame for the past is less important than taking charge of shaping the future.

Practice Wisdom and the Change Process

Change requires a sufficiently receptive environment.

You can stop big, but you usually have to start small.

You have four choices when facing a problem situation.

Three basic attitudes govern a challenging situation:
defeat, survival, or success.

Change takes time—something we know but assume doesn't apply to our change effort.

The fact that something makes sense has very little bearing on what happens.

The secret to life is good timing.

A moderate challenge is better than those that are too hard or too easy.

Pay due regard to the three Holy M's: the message, the medium, and the market.

On a good day the world operates 65% on form and 35% on substance.

You don't need to suggest a solution to identify a problem.

Your actions may well create discomfort.

A change that is put in place may not stay in place.

The work of community change is really the work of small groups.

It may be easier than you think.

How You Relate to People

Prevent yourself from contracting the disease of being right.

Listen as aggressively as you speak.

Declare your needs in a way that people can act on them.

You can't hold people accountable for things they don't know.

Don't bad-mouth people.

If you allow people to let you do all the work, they probably will.

Avoid taking up too much room in a conversation or in the action of the group.

How You Look at the Challenge of Change

Take the world as it is, not as it should be—then move it to where it should be.

Accept the fact of certain conditions, not the inevitability of them.

How You Relate to the Change Effort

If the issue is important, you will have to *act* as if it is.

To say "yes" to something is to say "no" to something else.

Pick the hills you're going to fight on.

Be willing to be surprised.

We create dragons that we then have to slay.

Don't set arbitrary limits on yourself.

Understand that your purpose is to be effective.

Pay attention to the keys to personal effectiveness.

General Self-Awareness

We all fall victim to listening for things we want to hear.

Be aware of whose interests you are protecting.

Avoid making excuses.

The moment you believe you are powerless you will indeed be powerless.

Look forward to some dessert.

Improving Your Effectiveness

If you don't know where you're going, you probably won't get there.

Ask forgiveness, not permission.

Don't ask, "Can we?" Ask, "*How* can we?"

If people agree, your best strategy is to shut up.

Follow up and follow through.

Pay attention to details.

Never assume that your interests are unimportant to important people.

Get your facts straight.

Don't just think about doing things, do them.

Observe the rule of the final inch.

Tactical Considerations

Use appropriate channels.

Hold people accountable, and keep the pressure on.

Push the discomfort upward.

Be willing to do the unexpected.

You will often need to dramatize the issue.

Pick an actionable issue.

Create options for mutual gain.

Engaging Resistance and Developing Support

Don't underestimate your opponent.

Give your opponents their proper due.

If you treat people as if they are allies, they are more likely to become allies; if you treat them as enemies, they are more likely to become enemies.

Always ask: "Who else should we be talking to?"

Identify stakeholders and develop investors in the change.

Put things in people's frames of reference and attention.

Link those who need to know with those who do know.

Keep people involved with the effort involved with each other.

Hold mutual and high expectations for people with whom you are working.

Look for ways to build commitment from people.

Create and Fill Key Roles Within the Organization

Formalize the role of the Nag.

Fill the role of the facilitator.

Make use of a Notifier.

Find a spark plug.

Strengthening Your Organization

Tasks need to be clear, manageable, and related.

Use time wisely; it is a resource in limited supply.

Your change effort better travel with a spare tire.

Stand back every now and then to look at things.

Don't start with the most important thing; start with the most interesting thing.

Meetings that produce nothing but future meetings are the death of the movement.

Work to develop capability, not just to solve problems.

Play to your strengths.

Keep your edge.

Understand the action–involvement–communication–decision cycle of empowerment.

Most People Have a Desire to Be Helpful

People are basically good and want to do good things; if given half a chance, they will.

People are willing to provide help, given the right circumstances.

People are willing to do things, but they just can't seem to start.

Each person has something to contribute.

Recognizing the Roles of Acceptance and Confidence

People want to be accepted and liked.

People need to feel worthy and able, competent and confident.

People need acknowledgment more than they need agreement.

People need to save face.

Recognize Common Human Traits That Must Be Taken Into Account

People hear selectively and remember what suits them.

People need to feel connected with others yet prized for their uniqueness.

People want freedom and direction, simultaneously.

People can see only what their vantage point allows them to see.

People are open to influence when they are distracted.

People are less open to influence when they have been inoculated against it.

People don't like to think their time is being wasted, especially by someone else.

Under stress people may vent their frustrations on the nearest available object.

All human behavior is designed to meet needs and is purposeful, not accidental.

Recognizing Matters That Lead to Inaction

Fear of losing what has been granted by those in power can lead people to docility.

When people are confused, they say no.

People run out of gas.

People are intimidated by the prospect of having to do it all.

People find security in their routines.

Lots of people will not ask for help.

Getting People Moving Toward Action and Keeping Them Going

If people cannot feel anything, they won't do anything.

Fear of the discomfort of disappointment can be more powerful than discomfort with the present situation.

People need to be sufficiently uncomfortable or sufficiently excited before they will take action.

People need to believe in the possibility of a successful outcome to take action.

People tend to take things more seriously when they are accountable to other people.

People tend to wait until the last minute to get things done.

People need to see immediate results to keep going.

People relate far better to a problem with which they have had a direct, personal experience.

To take action you need people; to get people you need action; changes result from the actions of people.

Recommended Readings

Over the years my own thinking has been influenced by the work of many activists and scholars. This reading list is representative of some of this work. I urge you to take advantage of this knowledge. It will strengthen your understanding of the field of community change.

Alinsky, S. D. (1972). *Rules for radicals: A pragmatic primer for realistic radicals.* New York: Random House

Berkowitz, W. R. (1982). *Community impact: Creating grassroots change in hard times.* Cambridge, MA: Schenkman.

Bobo, K., Kendall, J., & Max, S. (1996). *Organizing for social change: A manual for activists in the 1990's* (2nd ed.). Santa Ana, CA: Seven Locks Press.

Brager, G., & Holloway, S. (1978). *Changing human service organizations: Politics and practice.* New York: Free Press.

Burkey, S. (1993). *People first: A guide to self-reliant, participatory rural development.* Atlantic Highlands, NJ: Zed Books.

Cowan, G., & Egan, M. (1979). *People in systems: A model for development in the human-service professions and education.* Pacific Grove, CA: Brooks/Cole.

Fisher, R., & Ury, W. (1991). *Getting to yes: Negotiating without giving in* (2nd ed.). Boston, MA: Houghton Mifflin.

Friere, P. (1970). *Pedagogy of the oppressed.* New York: Continuum Press.

Friere, P. (1973). *Education for critical consciousness.* New York: Seabury.

Homan, M. S. (1999). *Promoting community change: Making it happen in the real world* (2nd ed.). Pacific Grove, CA: Brooks/Cole.

Johnson, D. W., & Johnson, F. P. (1997). *Joining together: Group theory and group skills* (6th ed.). Englewood Cliffs, NJ: Prentice-Hall.

Kahn, S. (1991). *Organizing: A guide for grassroots leaders* (rev. ed.). Silver Spring, MD: National Association of Social Workers.

Kahn, S. (1994). *How people get power* (rev. ed.). Washington, DC: National Association of Social Workers.

Kettner, P. M., Daley, J. M., & Nichols, A. W. (1985). *Initiating change in organizations and communities: A macro practice model.* Pacific Grove, CA: Brooks/Cole.

Kramer, R., & Specht, H. (1983). *Readings in community organization practice* (3rd ed.). Englewood Cliffs, NJ: Prentice-Hall.

Kretzman, J. P., & McNight, J. L. (1993). *Building communities from the inside out.* Chicago, IL: ACTA Publications.

Lappe, F. M., & Du Bois, P. M. (1994). *The quickening of America: Rebuilding our nation, remaking our lives.* San Francisco, CA: Jossey-Bass.

Lofquist, W. A. (1996). *The technology of development: A framework for transforming community cultures.* Tucson, AZ: Development Publications.

MacEachern, D. (1994). *Enough is enough! A hell-raiser's guide to community activism.* New York: Avon.

Marger, M. (1997). *Race and ethnic relations* (4th ed.). Belmont, CA: Wadsworth.

Mondross, J. B., & Wilson, S. M. (1994). *Organizing for power and empowerment.* New York: Columbia University Press.

Napier, R. W., & Gershenfeld, M. K. (1993). *Groups: Theory and experience* (5th ed.). Boston, MA: Houghton Mifflin.

O. M. Collective. (1971). *The organizers manual.* New York: Bantam Books.

Pertschuk, M. (1986). *Giant killers.* New York: Norton.

Putnam, R. D. (1995, Jan.). Bowling alone: America's declining social capital. *Journal of Democracy, 6*(1), 65–78.

Richan, W. C., & Mendelsohn, A. R. (1973). *Social work: The unloved profession.* New York: New Viewpoints.

Rivera, F., & Erlich, J. (1998). *Community organizing in a diverse society* (3rd ed.). Boston, MA: Allyn & Bacon.

Ronnby, A. (1995). *Mobilizing local communities.* Aldershot/Brookfield, USA/Hong Kong/Singapore/Sydney: Avebury.

Rothman, J., Erlich, J. L., & Tropman, J. E. (1995). *Strategies of community intervention* (5th ed.). Itasca, IL: F. E. Peacock. (All editions of this book of readings are helpful.)

Rothman, J., & Tropman, J. (1987). Models of community organization and macro practice perspectives: Their mixing and phasing. In F. M. Cox, J. L. Erlich, J. Rothman, & J. E. Tropman (Eds.), *Strategies of community organization: Macro practice* (4th ed.). (pp. 3–26). Itasca, IL: F. E. Peacock.

Rubin, H., & Rubin, I. (1991). *Community organizing and development.* Columbus, OH: Charles E. Merrill.

Schindler-Rainman, E. (1977). Goals to action. In E. Schindler-Rainman, R. Lippitt, & J. Cole (Eds.), *Taking your meetings out of the doldrums.* La Jolla, CA: University Associates, Inc.

Sharp, G. (1973). *The politics of nonviolent action. Part two: The methods of nonviolent action.* Boston, MA: Porter Sargent.

Shield, K. (1994). *In the tiger's mouth: An empowerment guide for social action.* Philadelphia, PA: New Society.

Staples, L. (1984). *Roots to power: A manual for grassroots organizing.* New York: Praeger.

Tropman, J. E., Cox, F., Erlich, J. L., & Rothman, J. (Eds.). (1995). *Tactics and techniques of community intervention* (3rd ed.). Itasca, IL: F. E. Peacock. (All editions of this book of readings are useful.)

Tuckman, B. W., & Jensen, M. A. C. (1977). Stages of small group development revisited. *Group and Organizational Studies, 2*(4), 419–427.

Williams, M. R. (1989). *Neighborhood organizing for urban school reform.* New York: Teachers College Press.

TO THE OWNER OF THIS BOOK:

I hope that you have found *Rules of the Game: Lessons from the Field of Community Change* useful. So that this book can be improved in a future edition, would you take the time to complete this sheet and return it? Thank you.

1. How did you acquire this book? _____

_____

_____

2. What did you like *most* about *Rules of the Game*? _____

_____

_____

_____

3. What did you like *least* about the book? _____

_____

_____

_____

4. In the space below, or on a separate sheet of paper, please write specific suggestions for improving this book and anything else you'd care to share about your experience in using the book.

_____

_____

_____

_____

_____

_____

Optional:

Your name: _____ Date: _____

May Brooks/Cole quote you, either in promotion for *Rules of the Game: Lessons from the Field of Community Change* or in future publishing ventures?

    Yes: _____ No: _____

    Sincerely,

    Mark S. Homan

FOLD HERE

FOLD HERE